Solo Travel, Tourism and Loneliness

This timely and topical book presents a unique critical exploration of the sociology of single travel and theory of consumption in relation to loneliness and tourism.

Logically structured and interdisciplinary in scope, this book introduces disrupting questions around the convergence of the post-modern self in relation to solo travel post-pandemic, with chapters exploring topics such as romantic loneliness, the benefits and drawbacks of single travel in a globalized world, the influence of technology on solo travel and the impact of sex tourism. International case studies and examples are given throughout and the book is richly illustrated and data-led. The volume looks to the future, exploring relevant trends and the development of new products and services in the next few years.

This volume is a pivotal resource for students, scholars and academics with an interest in tourism and mobility studies, international relations, development economics, crisis management, sociology and public policy. The book may also be of professional interest to practitioners and policymakers dedicated to tourism sociology and sociology of tourism consumption.

Hugues Séraphin is an Assistant Professor at Oxford Brookes University, United Kingdom.

Maximiliano E. Korstanje is an Associate Professor of Sociology at the University of Palermo, Argentina.

Routledge Focus on Tourism and Hospitality

Routledge Focus on Tourism and Hospitality presents small books on big topics and how they intersect with the world of tourism and hospitality research. The idea is to fill the gap between journal article and book. This new short form series offers both established and early-career academics the flexibility to publish cutting-edge commentary on key areas of tourism and hospitality, topical issues, policy-focused research, analytical or theoretical innovations, a summary of the key players or short topics for specialized audiences in a succinct way.

Mountaineering Tourism
A Critical Perspective
Michal Apollo and Yana Wengel

Managing People in Commercial Kitchens
A Contemporary Approach
*Charalampos Giousmpasoglou, Evangelia Marinakou,
Anastasios Zopiatis and John Cooper*

Smart Tourism Destination Governance
Technology and Design-Based Approach
Tomáš Gajdošík

Solo Travel, Tourism and Loneliness
A Critical Sociology
Hugues Séraphin and Maximiliano E. Korstanje

For more information about this series, please visit: https://www.routledge.com/tourism/series/FTH

Solo Travel, Tourism and Loneliness

A Critical Sociology

**Hugues Séraphin and
Maximiliano E. Korstanje**

Routledge
Taylor & Francis Group
LONDON AND NEW YORK

First published 2025
by Routledge
4 Park Square, Milton Park, Abingdon, Oxon OX14 4RN

and by Routledge
605 Third Avenue, New York, NY 10158

Routledge is an imprint of the Taylor & Francis Group, an informa business

© 2025 Hugues Séraphin and Maximiliano E. Korstanje

The right of Hugues Séraphin and Maximiliano E. Korstanje to be identified as authors of this work has been asserted in accordance with sections 77 and 78 of the Copyright, Designs and Patents Act 1988.

British Library Cataloguing-in-Publication Data
A catalogue record for this book is available from the British Library

ISBN: 978-1-032-81710-1 (hbk)
ISBN: 978-1-032-82108-5 (pbk)
ISBN: 978-1-003-50297-5 (ebk)

DOI: 10.4324/9781003502975

Typeset in Times New Roman
by codeMantra

Contents

Figures

Tables

1 Single Travel and Romantic Loneliness within the Sociology of Tourism

1.1 Introduction

From its outset, social sciences have remained a bit sceptical regarding the advance as well as the maturation of tourism as an emerging discipline. The founding parents of sociology (i.e. Durkheim and his L'Année Sociologique) have undermined the role played by leisure in the formation of social bondage. Norbert Elias was one of the pioneering voices to understand leisure as the glue of society. Malinowski´s preliminary ethnographies showed amply how Aborigine cultures developed pre-modern forms of leisure practices and geographical displacements. Like tourism, the question of play occupied a central position in Malinowski´s legacy. While sociology kept a positive viewpoint of leisure practices as a naïve (ideologised) activity centred on consumption and selfish behaviour, anthropology went further articulating seminal texts that paved the pathways for the rise of tourism anthropology (Korstanje & Seraphin, 2017). Today, sociology and anthropology – though keeping different angles – focus on tourism as their main object of study (Dann & Cohen, 1991; Apostolopoulos, Leivadi & Yiannakis, 2013; Cohen & Cohen, 2019). Tourism sociology has changed its research direction at the time. Scott Cohen & Eric Cohen enumerate seven different patterns the sub-discipline has followed since the 1960s: emotions, sensory experiences, materiality, gender, ethics, authentication and philosophical groundings of tourism theory. Although these categories, from being sufficient, are broader to be applied empirically, authors call attention to the role played by authenticity historically accompanied by knowledge production and the epistemology of tourism research. Authenticity, doubtless, is still the cornerstone of tourism sociology (Cohen & Cohen, 2019).

In the present chapter, we explain with accuracy the ebbs and flows of tourism sociology with a focus on the phenomenological dilemma of experience. The present chapter can be read in three separate parts. The first one is oriented to discuss the main (preliminary) contributions of two senior sociologists who have notably gravitated in the field, Dean MacCannell and Daniel Boorstin. Inherited from the old French structuralism, both envisaged a negative connotation of modern tourism. In the second part, we put in dialogue

DOI: 10.4324/9781003502975-1

part of French structuralism with the British cultural studies, above all with Lancaster School and the works authored by John Urry, Kevin Meethan, Keith Hollinshead, Jillian Ryckly-Boyd and Tim Edensor.

1.2   Sociology of Tourism

1.2.1   A Short Companion

It is safe to say that Daniel Boorstin and Dean MacCannell have made a notable contribution to the understanding of tourism in the academic circles of sociologists. Of course, Boorstin (1964) elicited a caustic critique of mass tourism in synch with French philosophy. To understand Boorstin´s works, it is necessary to come back to the roots of French philosophy, an academic movement that developed a pejorative conception of leisure and tourism. In consonance with this, Boorstin (1964) holds a more than polemic thesis; tourism is a degenerative (denigrated) mode of travel based on the combination of recent technological breakthroughs and the consolidation of consumerist society. Tourists – far from being engaged with locals – look to gaze (consume) pseudo-experiences fabricated and commoditised for them. What is more important, tourists are often limited to consuming *pseudo-events* (he ultimately dubbed as *cultural dopes*). Rather, Dean MacCannell offers a more sophisticated (if not elaborated) argument. Most certainly, MacCannell is mostly influenced by Durkhemian and Levistraussian structuralism. For MacCannell, tourism should be seen as something more important than a commercial activity or an industry. Without any doubt, tourism is the glue of society. Echoing the original Durkheim´s ideas around the *tribal totem,* MacCannell argues convincingly that tourism not only sublimates social frustrations but also keeps society united. In aboriginal (pre-modern) organisations, the political authority of chiefdom emanates from the symbolism of totem. The social ties are conditioned by the sphere of sacredness while the totem is defined as a reflection of the group or clan consciousness. Having said this, in the modern lifestyle, the totem cedes to the figure of tourism. Far from being a pseudo-travel (like in Boorstin), in MacCannell tourism has a double function. Tourists – as agents – look to consume authentic experience, but paradoxically, in so doing, this yearned authenticity becomes a staged authenticity. Once transformed into consumers, tourists freely move to gaze at a fabricated world previously reified to meet all consumers´ expectancies. In the meantime, MacCannell will change his stance radicalising his argument. Tourists avoid socialising with other tourists because their travels take part in empty meeting grounds (MacCannell, 1973, 1976, 2002a, 2002b).

1.2.2   Tourism Sociology Today

To sum up almost four decades of production in a section seems to be a task very hard to grasp. We here also describe the main epistemological guidelines of enquiry of tourism sociology revolving on two specific topics: authenticity and the aversion to interacting with 'other tourists'. This begs a more than important question: what is authenticity?

Over the years, authenticity has eloquently created a controversial background within the academic tribes (Hughes, 1995; Olsen, 2002; Rickly-Boyd, 2022). Scott Cohen and Eric Cohen alert that in tourism sociology the problem of authenticity lies in the heterogeneity of modern society which is based on simple binaries: authentic-inauthentic. Some interesting works have emphasised on the lazy empathy (engagement) of tourists with local culture. This *lazy empathy* does not involve the self with the visited landscape. Hence authenticity – as a main concept – cannot be divorced from the tourist experience, and of course, experiences take place in meeting places. What is equally important, since these encounters are performed in multicultural sites (or climates of hybridisation) ethics is particularly important. To some extent, ethics has little application because of the advance of cultural relativism. To some extent, sociology asks to answer how travel behaviour can be ethically regulated when travellers do not share the same ethical norms as hosting countries. As a global force, tourism confronts local habits or customs putting the future of multiculturalism into the foreground. It is important to mention that in quest of authentic experiences, tourists breach the local laws. The question of authenticity cannot be understood without performativity; to put the same in other terms, authenticity results from a symbolic construction entirely legitimated by what ethnographers dubbed role performativity. Given the problem in these terms, what is authentic or not depends upon the role of the gazer (or consumer) (Cohen & Cohen, 2019). Authenticity makes stronger in contexts of relational transformation (Tucker, 2019; Swain, 2009; Tzanelli, 2015). In this respect, Keith Hollinshead uses the term *world-making or world-making authority* to denote the complex coexistence of different phenomenological worlds revolving around the same linguistic representation. Axiomatically, beyond the individual perceptions various worlds are representable and conceivable in linguistics. The world-making process is symbolised by the convergence of power and politics. The term, which was originally coined by Nelson Goodman, was introduced by Hollingshead in the fields of tourism, to describe how cultures and places are drawn by tourism. Per Hollingshead, the process of world-making can be used to foster a creative authority in constructing specific-based forms of locality. The world-making process activates a social imaginary that orchestrates representational repertoires of subjects, storylines, and sites. At first glimpse, since world-making activates a deep interpretation of local culture, tourists should be understood as something more complex than docile consumers or pleasure-seekers. Tourists are often agents that penetrate, negotiate and internalise reality. In this vein, tourism acts as a key driver in its ability to transform places, landscapes and cultures, articulating all-encompassing modes of surveillance. Most plausibly, the power of tourism does not rest on its capacity to homogenise the world but in its capacity to transform local moods (Hollinshead, 1992, 1998, 2006, 2009; Hollinshead, Ateljevic & Ali, 2009). Hollingshead's Worldmaking can be well homologised to what John Urry named as tourist gaze. Likewise, Urry starts from the premise that the tourist gaze is simply circumscribed to a deep cultural matrix that says what can be gazed upon or not. Urry divides the geographical landscape into two types, wild or risky zones, and civilised areas (which include tourist destinations, shopping malls as well and leisure spots). As part of the net of experts, tour operators offer a cognitive map that suggests what destinations should be visited or avoided (Lash & Urry, 1993; Urry, 2002; Urry & Larsen, 2011). Farfetched as it may sound, Urry toys with the belief that there should be a point of enquiry between cultural theory – which was widely explored – and the advances of post-Marxism. In sharp contrast to MacCannell, Urry holds that tourists (as active agents) negotiate and interrogate the supra-structural constructions (Rojek & Urry, 1997). In Bauman's terms, tourists can delay instant gratification while gaining further autonomy in their decision-making process. The free-choice, in a society of consumption, sets the pace for the rise of a privileged class that is legally encouraged to tour the world. The opposite is equally true, those who are relegated from the formal labour market conform to a new infra-class – Bauman mentions as vagabonds (Bauman, 1996, 1998, 2000). Let's return for a moment to Urry; tourism moves in a new aesthetic re-flexibility dominated by the power of the sign. In this emerging stage, tourists, cultures, merchandise and landscapes are commoditised as products (Rojek & Urry, 1997).

The same point of concern can be found in another British Senior philosopher, Kevin Meethan. If MacCannell sustained the arguments of French structuralism stressing alienation, as well as Urry recurring to the cultural theory to understand modern mobility, Meethan goes in another direction. With the benefits of hindsight, Meethan acknowledges the irreversible expansion of the capitalist system, but alerting that this process moulds permeable geographical borders and social identities. Based on the City of York as the main study case, he holds that authenticity plays a marginal role in the configuration of the modern tourism industry. Fieldworkers should understand that tourism and consumption are inextricably intertwined. Both forces – from different levels – work together to optimise human pleasure. Consumption greases the rails of new experiences while keeping the consumer's identity. Fluidity, not authenticity, sets the pace of global modernity. As he puts it, even if the patterns of consumption have been gradually changed, the change seems to be irreversible. The advance of tourism has offered new forms of decoding local cultures. The formation of identities and cultures is more fluid than at other times. In the field of tourism, at least, the spectacle is culturally framed by the dominant (European) ideologies. However, tourists – unlike other types of consumers – should go away from home to materialise their consumption process. In consonance with Urry, he said overtly that there is a cultural matrix that conditions the tourist experience, but this matrix is consolidated by tourist behaviour and the identity cemented by the (mass) media. Most certainly, tourism revives a constant negotiation with the 'Other', where the consumer recreates their own identity. This negotiation takes place by exchanging experiences and emotions. As he adheres, consumers are not active players, but docile receptors of marketing and ad campaigns. To wit, the tourist experience is externally designed to be adjusted to the consumers' cosmologies. Meethan strongly believes not only MacCannell but also Urry took the incorrect way. This happened because neither Marxism nor structuralism suffices to explain the so-called selectivity of consumers in a hybridised world. This selectivity is given by the combination of two factors, co-production-consumption and interpretation. While the former signals the process of producing while consuming, the latter refers to the ways this process is formed and ultimately exchanged. What seems to be more important, tourism alters the sense of place reproducing proper disengaged narratives of self. Tourism carves deeply into the history each generation builds. From generation to generation, the local culture is pervaded and interpreted through the demand generated by tourism. Last but not least, modernity operates in a climate of circularity where local culture is daily transformed. This process was identified and consequently baptised by Meethan as the *genealogy of tourism*. Citizens do not live in a mobile culture, rather they are psychologically moved to find new experiences. This quest for 'Otherness' opens the doors to a self-discovery that mediates between normalcy and exoticness. Humans wander all their lives in quest of a home, but once found, they need space. This metaphor helps in understanding the host-guests' relationships. Tourists, at least initially, are not passive receptors who look to maximise their pleasure, or so to speak reduce their pain but technology (or the media) packages and standardises the experience earlier it takes room. As a result of this, consumers do not move freely in quest of an authentic interaction with locals, or other tourists, they travel alone in their imagined narrative (Meethan, 1996, 2003, 2004, 2006, 2014).

As the previous argument is given, Tim Edensor and Jillian Rickly-Boyd give an interesting snapshot to complement the early-discussed axioms. Rickly Boyd traces back her line of enquiry to the tourist performance. It is safe to say her goals are twofold. On one hand, she tries updating the existing literature to form a new geographically informed theory of tourism. To some extent, she lays the epistemological foundations to describe how the sense of place is formed, exchanged, and internalised. On another, she builds a fertile (if not critical) dialogue with American anthropologist Dean MacCannell. Centred on Peircean semiotics, she argues convincingly one of the main contradictions of tourism sociology has been the separation between the tourist sites and the tourist practices. Per her viewpoint, tourism should be contemplated as a liminoid ritual articulated to transform the visited place, local cultures, and the connection with the 'Other'. Hence tourism should be studied considering how these rituals are performed in the place. As she concludes, MacCannell has shed light on the problem of authenticity and rituality, but his theory was limited to the act of sightseeing. Designed as a social institution, tourism facilitates much deeper rituals to foster social integration and solidarity (Rickly-Boyd, Knudsen & Braverman, 2016; Rickly-Boyd, 2009; Knudsen & Rickly-Boyd, 2012).

Tim Edensor´s approach seems to be similar to Rickly-Boyd´s thesis, so to speak at a surface. In a seminal paper entitled *Staging Tourism* which was originally published in the Annals of Tourism Research in 2000, Edensor pays his attention to the fact the literature has emphasised the archetype of tourists as performers who move in different dimensions. The motivation behind these tourists is the key driver of the current tourism research. In this token, tourists interact with the landscape in different ways whether they travel alone or in groups. Edensor reminds us that tourist behaviour is culturally determined by how the travel is performed. Unlike his colleagues, Edensor focuses strictly in the matter of politics and the narratives of power. In so doing, he distinguishes the *enclavic tourism from heterogeneous tourism*. The industry has evolved according these two paradigms. While enclave tourism appealed to create a symbolic barrier (bubble) to avoid host-guests interactions, a global force marked by heterogeneity resulted finally in postmodern (or multicultural) tourism. However both forces are sides of the same coin. One of the problems of tourism sociology rests on the imposition of abstract categorisations that obscure more than they clarify. In consonance with that, tourism should be re-conceptualised as an ongoing process aimed to reconstruct the social praxis. At a closer look, this social praxis is strongly regulated by key personnel who scrutinise social agents' interactions. For that reason, the ruling class can inculcate embodied customs through the instrumentalisation of ritual performance. The hegemony should be thought of as something more than a part of politics or power, it decodes the meanings of a world that remains unknown to us. To put the same bluntly,

'While dominant rules and principles often hold sway, performances vary enormously and depend upon the regulation of the stage and the players, and the relationship between the players. Rather than being fixed, performance is an interactive and contingent process: it succeeds according to the skill of the actors, the context within which it is performed, and how it is interpreted by an audience. Even the most delineated social performance must be re-enacted in different conditions and its reception cannot always be controlled by the performer. Since no separate performance can ever be exactly reproduced, fixity of meaning must be continually strived for'.

(Edensor, 2000: 324)

Having said this, Edensor enumerates tourism performance in different dimensions. The tourist practices are enmeshed into a set of countless discourses and practical orientations. Tourists often move through specific spaces but oscillate into a vast spectrum of interpretations. The same visitor may very well have different interpretations of the place in different moments of its life. Tourists are more than consumers they move as their historically constituted biographies. Anyway, he finds some rules that traverse the tourist performance. The first one speaks to us of the fact that *all performances are socially located in time and space.* Social performance is circumscribed to the historical connection of people with the visited place. Emulating ritualistic patterns, tourists desire to perform a new role escaping from the humdrum routine. Tourists emulate to be what they are not in daily life. Social and spatial regulations are controlled through many theatrical metaphors that organise the tourist gaze. Instrumentally, Edensor not only returns to discuss Urry's axioms but also coins a neologism, tourist gardens. Tourists, far from moving freely, are choreographed to move during certain circles, routes, and borders controlled by the gatekeepers or police of the gardens. Lastly, the notion of performance is given by competence. Tourists perform roles in which they have been skilled and trained. They rarely interact with other tourists simply because each tourist should reproduce their performance (Edensor, 2000, 2001, 2006, 2007). To here we have reviewed a part of tourism sociology literature regarding the concept of authenticity and the interaction with other tourists. In the next section, we will detail to what extent the literature should be updated according to the new times.

1.2.3 The Future of Tourism Sociology

The sociology of tourism has advanced a lot in recent decades. As a sub-discipline, it encompassed a set of diverse theories and ranges of study which includes hosts-guest interaction or conflicts (Smith, 1989; Graburn, 1983), Social imaginaries (Salazar & Graburn, 2014), hybridisation or acculturation process (Cohen, 1984), neo-colonial discourses (Comaroff & Comaroff, 2009), effects of the industry on the local culture, as well as roles, motivations and tourists' relationships with locals or other tourists (Dann & Cohen, 1991; Uriely, 2001; Sharpley, 2018). Over recent years, some bibliometric studies attempted to explain the gravitation of tourism sociology in the field of sociology. The obtained results showed a marginal contribution of tourism sociology to classic sociology (Xiao & Smith, 2006; Benckendorff & Zehrer, 2013). Henceforth, Cohen and Cohen (2019) have called attention to imagining new constellations for tourism sociology in the next decades. At the same time, Donna Chambers and Tijana Rakic (2015) urge tourism sociologists to throw out the intellectual bathwater while salving the baby. As they lament, the existent critical turn in tourism sociology intends to eradicate the bases of tourism sociology. Although the discipline has entered into a type of postmodern crisis, no less true seems to be that tourism sociology pivoted in the imagination of new topics.

1.3   Solo Tourism in the Twenty-first Century

After the breakout of COVID-19, the number of solo travellers increased significantly, particularly from travellers from the United States, Australia, the United Kingdom and Canada (Solo Traveler World, 2023). However, the cost travelling following the pandemic negatively impacted the mobility of solo travellers who are more and more looking for cheaper options (Mulvey, Padgett & Lever, 2022; Agustina & Sharyputra, 2022).

Postmodern sociology applied to the study of solo tourism situates as one of the promising topics fleshed out in the present book. Solo tourism has received a dual interpretation which is summed up in the following question. Is solo tourism a new niche or tendency that illustrates new types of travel behaviour or simply a clear sign of social ties decomposition?

Tourism sociology is carved on the intersection of social ties decomposition and solo tourism. For some critical voices, solo tourism represents a selfish tendency developed by alienation and individualism (Jordan & Aitchison, 2008; Alfredo, 2001). We are moving, doubtless, to an individual (fragmented) society. What is more important, technology mediates between individuals and their emotional relationships (Tonkis, 2003). However, the discrepancy is far from being closed. Some studies have found interesting results that evince solo travel or romantic tourism as are expression of engagement with 'Others' and reciprocity (Pritchard, 2007; Molz, 2012; Pereira & Silva, 2018; Bianchi, 2022). As Craig Leith (2020) puts it, there is a notable increase in *solo life choices* or people living alone. This loner living has been identified as a global trend that transcends all Western cultures. The reasons behind these decisions include greater employment movement or time, individual preferences (lifestyles), as well as higher divorce rates. Nowadays, solo tourism is a growing niche formed by individuals going on holidays alone. In some cases, this niche preferably travels alone though it joins a tour group later. As the authors acknowledge, solo travellers should not be stigmatised as selfish consumers, but as people who are looking for new ways of relationships, or consumers associated with the search of solicitude. There is a clear distinction between loneliness and solicitude. While the former is based on the lack of choice to be or not alone, the latter signals an individual (temporal) decision to travel alone to get specific experiences. The potential of solo tourism, as a fertile ground for future research, seems to be at least palpable. Manthiou, Luong and Klaus (2023) conceptualise solo tourism as a new tendency, accelerated by the COVID-19 pandemic, of self-discovery legitimated in slow or well-being tourism. Seow and Brown (2020) alert that solo travel can be juxtaposed with gender asymmetries. While men are legally encouraged to consume these types of products, solo women travellers are stigmatised or subject to global risks. As a result of this, they should be involved in attacks, sexual harassment, or even abuse. These worries are coincident with studies such as Yang, Yang and Khoo-Lattimore (2019), Jordan and Gibson (2005),

Wilson and Little (2005), McNamara and Prideaux (2010), and Wantono and McKercher (2020), only to name a few. The correlation between gender and risk perception in solo tourism is mainly a matter of perception (Lepp & Gibson, 2003; Kaba, 2021). Individual perceptions or narratives emanating from the visited destination are key factors that explain why many women solo travellers select exotic destinations – despite the cultural barriers (Kaba, 2021; Yang, 2016). To the best of our knowledge, the best example is the COVID-19 pandemic. Many travellers adopted this new custom to feel safer from a potential infection with this lethal virus (Bert et al., 2020; Matsuura & Saito, 2022). In consonance with this, Lynn Jonas (2022) calls attention to the long-dormant anxieties wakened up by the recent COVID-19. The imposition of strict lockdowns, with the lemma stay at home, disposed of by governments to stop the virus has wreaked havoc not only in the tourism industry but also in changing travel behaviour. Solo tourism became in safer travel option for persons reluctant to interact with others because of health issues. COVID-19 introduced the question of social distancing to avoid the contagion. In this context, solo tourism is widely valorised as a healthier and safer alternative for a great portion of the tourist demand. The potential of this niche is prone to the dismantling of stigma along with the act of travelling alone.

Even if solo travellers are not systematically single, most of them are (Chiang & Jogaratnam, 2005; Kim & Jang, 2017; Yang et al., 2019), particularly women (Ghai & Chowdhri, 2022). On that basis, this book is arguing that solo travellers can be associated with single travel. To be more explicit and to keep it simple, this book is arguing that single travellers are solo travellers.

1.4   Conclusion

It is tempting to say that tourism sociology has notably contributed to the advancement of tourism research. Although classic sociology was really oath to study leisure and tourism, the first sociologists of tourism started from a different concern. They had the plunge into tourism waters to understand to what extent tourism acted as an ideological instrument of domestication. Echoing their cue from critical French philosophy which bemoaned the advance of industrialism destroys the social ties, these pioneering voices developed a critical viewpoint of tourism. This seems to be a case of Daniel Boorstin who elicits an historical reading of travel. For Boorstin, tourism is fraught with pseudo-events designed to alienate the lay citizens. Since American anthropologist Dean MacCannell, tourism has been seen as a serious object of study. Although his structuralist viewpoint was widely criticised, MacCannell laid the epistemological foundations for a new tourism sociology theory. Important well-versed scholars such as John Urry, Tim Edensor, Kevin Meethan or even Keith Hollinshead devoted their time and efforts to decipher part of the open points left by MacCannell: what is authenticity and tourism consumption? Here the question of solidarity, engagement and experience occupied a central position in the evolution of the discipline. What seems to be equally important, tourism sociology was cemented on the concerns revolving around how authentic the tourist experience is. It is noteworthy that any tourist moves alone simply in quest of outstanding or unique experiences. The interaction with other tourists or even locals is based only on specific patterns that affirm the tourist's previous expectations. A scan of the literature suggests that tourists are subject to 'cultural narratives', a cultural matrix, or simply to worldmaking patterns, that mark how the interaction takes place. Lastly, a critical turn has been noted that the tourist experience is performed in the digital media before the consumer travels. As a result of this, solo travel and romantic tourism would be a clear sign of social decomposition. This moot point has wakened up serious discrepancies in countless studies. This and the rest of the chapters interrogate on the strengths and weaknesses of tourism sociology to explain solo travel with rigorous accuracy. Although Solo or single tourism has surfaced by countless reasons associated to the radical changes of modern lifestyles, no less true seems to be that this tendency came to stay after the pandemic.

To discuss single travellers, this book is focusing on their needs as consumers of both the tourism and hospitality industries. From the travel side, the focus is on the role and importance of travelling apps, particularly for women. From the hospitality side, the book is focusing on speed dating events. This type of product and service can not only meet the needs to single travellers when on only, but also when they are not. Destinations could for instance work with hospitality providers to offer speed dating as a tourism product and service, and subsequently address the issue of romantic loneliness (Part II).

Loneliness is a major societal issue related to depression (Van As et al., 2022), which affects a variety of members of the society, such as older people (Domènech-Abella et al., 2017), young adults (Matthews et al., 2016), people with illness (Gallagher, Bennett & Roper, 2021), etc. For instance, it affects 11 million adults in the UK, and particularly women (Champion Health, 2023). In most cases loneliness is investigated in terms of isolation, particularly when it comes to older people (Feng, Altinay & Alrawadieh, 2022; Fessman & Lester, 2000; Song & Qu, 2017; Van As et al., 2022). Romantic loneliness is very rarely investigated in academic literature regardless the field of study (Adamczyk, 2017, 2018; Seeparsad et al., 2008; Séraphin, 2023).

As for Part III, it explored the implications of single/solo travellers for the tourism and hospitality industries from practical and theoretical perspectives. Finally, the conclusion (Part IV), discusses the importance of sociology in tourism, as the field of study is made of concepts which are discursive formation, and as such are constantly changing (O'Regan et al., 2022).

References

Adamczyk, K. (2017). Voluntary and involuntary singlehood and young adults' mental health: An investigation of mediating role of romantic loneliness. *Current Psychology, 36,* 888–904. https://doi.org/10.1007/s12144-016-9478-3

Adamczyk, K. (2018). Direct and indirect effects of relationship status through unmet need to belong and fear of being single on young adults' romantic loneliness. *Personality and Individual Differences, 124,* 124–129. https://doi.org/10.1016/j. paid.2017.12.011

Agustina, N. K. W., & Sharyputra, D. (2022). Travel pattern and pandemic; How do travel preferences effects the changes in expenses in new normal era? *JurnalKepari-wisataan: Destinasi, Hospitalitas Dan Perjalanan, 6*(1), 96–106.

Alfredo, A. (2001). Geography of tourism-the ecological crisis as an objective criticism of labor. Tourism as a "necessary illusion". *GEOUSP Espaço e Tempo (Online), 5*(1), 37–62.

Apostolopoulos, Y., Leivadi, S., & Yiannakis, A. (2013). *The sociology of tourism: Theoretical and empirical investigations.* Abingdon: Routledge.

Bauman, Z. (1996). *Tourists and vagabonds: Heroes and victims of postmodernity.* Wien: Institut fur Hohere Studien.

Bauman, Z. (1998). On glocalization: Or globalization for some, localization for some others. *Thesis Eleven, 54*(1), 37–49.

Bauman, Z. (2000). *Liquid modernity.* Cambridge: Polity Press.

Benckendorff, P., & Zehrer, A. (2013). A network analysis of tourism research. *Annals of Tourism Research, 43,* 121–149.

Bert, J., Schellong, D., Hagenmaier, M., Hornstein, D., Wegscheider, A. K., & Palme, T. (2020). How COVID-19 will shape urban mobility. *City, 25*(28), 21–28.

Bianchi, C. (2022). Antecedents of tourists' solo travel intentions. *Tourism Review, 77*(3), 780–795.

Boorstin, D. J. (1964). *The image: A guide to pseudo-events in America.* New York: Harper & Row.

Chambers, D., & Rakic, T. (2015). *Tourism Research Frontiers: Beyond the boundaries of knowledge.* Bingley: Emerald.

Champion Health (2023). Depression statistics UK. Retrieved from https://champion-health.co.uk/insights/depression-statistics/

Chiang, C. Y., & Jogaratnam, G. (2005). Why do women travel solo for purposes of leisure? *Journal of Vacation Marketing, 12*(1), 59–70.

Cohen, E. (1984). The sociology of tourism: Approaches, issues, and findings. *Annual Review of Sociology, 10*(1), 373–392.

Cohen, S. A., & Cohen, E. (2019). New directions in the sociology of tourism. *Current Issues in Tourism, 22*(2), 153–172.

Comaroff, J. L., & Comaroff, J. (2009). *Ethnicity, inc* (p. 21). Chicago, IL: University of Chicago Press.

Dann, G., & Cohen, E. (1991). Sociology and tourism. *Annals of Tourism Research, 18*(1), 155–169.

Domènech-Abella, J., Lara, E., Rubio-Valera, M., et al. (2017). Loneliness and depression in the elderly: The role of social network. *Social Psychiatry and Psychiatric Epidemiology, 52,* 381–390. https://doi.org/10.1007/s00127-017-1339-3

Edensor, T. (2000). Staging tourism: Tourists as performers. *Annals of Tourism Research, 27*(2), 322–344.

Edensor, T. (2001). Performing tourism, staging tourism: (Re) producing tourist space and practice. *Tourist Studies*, *1*(1), 59–81.

Edensor, T. (2006). Sensing tourist spaces. In Minca, C., & Oakes, T. (Eds.), *Travels in paradox: Remapping tourism* (pp. 23–45). New York: Rowman & Littlefield.

Edensor, T. (2007). Mundane mobilities, performances and spaces of tourism. *Social & Cultural Geography*, *8*(2), 199–215.

Feng, K., Altinay, L., & Alrawadieh, Z. (2022). Social connectedness and well-being of elderly customers: Do employee-to-customer interactions matter? *Journal of Hospitality Marketing and Management*, *32*(2), 174–195.

Fessman, N., & Lester, D. (2000). Loneliness and depression among elderly nursing home patients. *The International Journal of Aging and Human Development*, *51*(2), 137–141. https://doi.org/10.2190/5VY9-N1VT-VBFX-50RG

Gallagher, S., Bennett, K. M., & Roper, L. (2021). Loneliness and depression in patients with cancer during COVID-19. *Journal of Psychosocial Oncology*, *39*(3), 445–451. https://doi.org/10.1080/07347332.2020.1853653

Ghai, A., & Chowdhri, S. (2022). Study on hotel trends designed for single lady travelers. *PUSA Journal of Hospitality and Applied Sciences*, *8*(1), 47–61.

Graburn, N. H. (1983). The anthropology of tourism. *Annals of Tourism Research*, *10*(1), 9–33.

Hollinshead, K. (1992). 'White' gaze, 'red' people—Shadow visions: The disidentification of 'Indians' in cultural tourism. *Leisure Studies*, *11*(1), 43–64.

Hollinshead, K. (1998). Tourism, hybridity, and ambiguity: The relevance of Bhabha's 'third space' cultures. *Journal of Leisure Research*, *30*(1), 121–156.

Hollinshead, K. (2006). The shift to constructivism in social inquiry: Some pointers for tourism studies. *Tourism Recreation Research*, *31*(2), 43–58.

Hollinshead, K. (2009). The "worldmaking" prodigy of tourism: The reach and power of tourism in the dynamics of change and transformation. *Tourism Analysis*, *14*(1), 139–152.

Hollinshead, K., Ateljevic, I., & Ali, N. (2009). Worldmaking agency–worldmaking authority: The sovereign constitutive role of tourism. *Tourism Geographies*, *11*(4), 427–443.

Hughes, G. (1995). Authenticity in tourism. *Annals of tourism Research*, *22*(4), 781–803.

Jonas, L. C. (2022). Solo tourism: A great excuse to practice social distancing. *African Journal of Hospitality, Tourism and Leisure*, *11*(SE1), 556–564.

Jordan, F., & Aitchison, C. (2008). Tourism and the sexualisation of the gaze: Solo female tourists' experiences of gendered power, surveillance and embodiment. *Leisure Studies*, *27*(3), 329–349.

Jordan, F., & Gibson, H. (2005). "We're not stupid… But we'll not stay home either": Experiences of solo women travelers. *Tourism Review International*, *9*(2), 195–211.

Kaba, B. (2021). Foreign solo female travellers' perceptions of risk and safety in Turkey. In Krevs, M. (Ed.), *Hidden Geographies* (pp. 475–493). New York: Springer Nature.

Kim, D. H., & Jang, S. C. (2017). Therapeutic benefits of dining out, traveling, and drinking: Coping strategies for lonely consumers to improve their mood. *International Journal of Hospitality Management*, *67*, 106–114. https://doi.org/10.1016/j.ijhm.2017.08.013

Knudsen, D. C., & Rickly-Boyd, J. M. (2012). Tourism sites as semiotic signs: A critique. *Annals of Tourism Research*, *39*(2), 1252–1254.

Korstanje, M., & Seraphin, H. (2017). Revisiting the sociology of consumption in tourism. In Dixit, K. (Ed.), *The Routledge handbook of consumer behaviour in hospitality and tourism* (pp. 16–25). Abingdon: Routledge.

Lash, S., & Urry, J. (1993). *Economies of signs and space* (Vol. 26). London: Sage.

Leith, C. (2020). Tourism trends: Lifestyle developments and the links to solo tourism. *Journal of Tourism Futures, 6*(3), 251–255.

Lepp, A., & Gibson, H. (2003). Tourist roles, perceived risk and international tourism. *Annals of Tourism Research, 30*(3), 606–624.

MacCannell, D. (1973). Staged authenticity: Arrangements of social space in tourist settings. *American Journal of Sociology, 79*(3), 589–603.

MacCannell, D. (1976). *The tourist: A new theory of the leisure class.* Berkeley: University of California Press.

MacCannell, D. (2002a). *Empty meeting grounds: The tourist papers.* Abingdon: Routledge.

MacCannell, D. (2002b). The ego factor in tourism. *Journal of Consumer research, 29*(1), 146–151.

Manthiou, A., Klaus, P., & Luong, V. H. (2022). Slow tourism: Conceptualization and interpretation–A travel vloggers' perspective. *Tourism Management, 93,* 104570.

Matsuura, T., & Saito, H. (2022). The COVID-19 pandemic and domestic travel subsidies. *Annals of Tourism Research, 92,* 103326.

Matthews, T., Danese, A., Wertz, J., Odgers, C. L., Ambler, A., Moffitt, T. E., & Arseneault, L. (2016). Social isolation, loneliness and depression in young adulthood: a behavioural genetic analysis. *Social Psychiatry and Psychiatric Epidemiology, 51,* 339–348.

McNamara, K. E., & Prideaux, B. (2010). A typology of solo independent women travellers. *International Journal of Tourism Research, 12*(3), 253–264.

Meethan, K. (1996). Consuming (in) the civilized city. *Annals of Tourism Research, 23*(2), 322–340.

Meethan, K. (2003). Mobile Cultures?, Hybridity, tourism and cultural change. *Journal of Tourism and Cultural Change, 1*(1), 11–28.

Meethan, K. (2004). To stand in the shores of my ancestors. In Coles, T., & Timothy, D. (Eds.), *Tourism, disaporas and space* (pp. 139–150). London: Routledge.

Meethan, K. (2006). Introduction: Narratives of place and self. In Meethan, K., Anderson, A., & Miles, S. (Eds.), *Tourism consumption and representation* (pp. 1–23). Wellingford: CABI.

Meethan, K. (2014). Mobilities, ethnicities and tourism. In Lew, A., Hall, M. C., & Williams, A. (Eds.), *Tourism* (pp. 240–250). New York: Wiley Blackwell.

Molz, J. G. (2012). *Travel connections: Tourism, technology and togetherness in a mobile world.* Abingdon: Routledge.

Mulvey, M. S., Padgett, D. T., & Lever, M. W. (2022). Sustaining travel dreams in retirement: Guidance at the crossroads. In Garcia, L. J., Bélanger-Hardy, L., Jutai, J. W., & Łuszczyńska, M. (Eds.), *Well-being in Later Life: The Notion of Connected Autonomy* (pp. 65–81). Abingdon: Routledge.

Olsen, K. (2002). Authenticity as a concept in tourism research: The social organization of the experience of authenticity. *Tourist Studies, 2*(2), 159–182.

O'Regan, M., Salazar, N. B., Choe, J., & Buhalis, D. (2022). Unpacking overtourism as a discursive formation through interdiscursivity. *Tourism Review, 77*(1), 54–71. https://doi.org/10.1108/TR-12-2020-0594

Pereira, A., & Silva, C. (2018). Women solo travellers: Motivations and experiences. *Millenium, 1* (6), 99–106.

Pritchard, A. (Ed.). (2007). *Tourism and gender: Embodiment, sensuality and experience.* Wallinford: Cabi.

Rickly-Boyd, J. M. (2009). Establishing authenticity in a tourist landscape: Spring Mill pioneer village. *Material Culture, 41*(1), 1–16.

Rickly-Boyd, J. M. (2022). A review of authenticity research in tourism: Launching the Annals of Tourism Research Curated Collection on authenticity. *Annals of Tourism Research, 92,* 103349.

Rickly-Boyd, J. M., Knudsen, D. C., & Braverman, L. C. (2016). *Tourism, performance, and place: A geographic perspective.* Abingdon: Routledge.

Rojek, C., & Urry, J. (Eds.). (1997). *Touring cultures.* Abingdon: Taylor & Francis.

Salazar, N. B., & Graburn, N. H. (Eds.). (2014). *Tourism imaginaries: Anthropological approaches.* Oxford: Berghahn books.

Seepersad, S., Choi, M. K., & Shin, N. (2008). How does culture influence the degree of romantic loneliness and closeness?. *The Journal of Psychology, 142*(2), 209–220.

Seow, D., & Brown, L. (2020). The solo female Asian tourist. *Current Issues in Tourism, 21*(10), 1187–1206, https://doi.org/10.1080/13683500.2017.1423283

Séraphin, H. (2023). 'Special Interest and Meso-Adultainment Events' as a New Type of Event to Existing Literature. *Journal of Convention & Events,* doi: 10.1080/15470148.2023.2209341

Sharpley, R. (2018). *Tourism, tourists and society.* Abingdon: Routledge.

Smith, V. L. (1989). *Hosts and guests: The anthropology of tourism.* Philadelphia: University of Pennsylvania Press.

Song, J., & Qu, H. (2017). How does consumer regulatory focus impact perceived value and consumption emotions? *International Journal of Contemporary Hospitality Management, 31*(1), 285–308.

Su, C. J. (2022). Post-pandemic studies in tourism and hospitality. *Service Business, 16*(3), 413–416.

Swain, M. B. (2009). The cosmopolitan hope of tourism: Critical action and worldmaking vistas. *Tourism Geographies, 11*(4), 505–525.

Tonkiss, F. (2003). The ethics of indifference: Community and solitude in the city. *International journal of cultural studies, 6*(3), 297–311.

Tucker, H. (2019). Colonialism and its tourism legacies. In Dallen, T. (Ed.), *Handbook of globalisation and tourism* (pp. 90–99). Cheltenham: Edward Elgar.

Tzanelli, R. (2015). *Mobility, modernity and the slum: The real and virtual journeys of 'Slumdog millionaire'.* Abingdon: Routledge.

Uriely, N. (2001). 'Travelling workers' and 'working tourists': Variations across the interaction between work and tourism. *International Journal of Tourism Research, 3*(1), 1–8.

Urry, J. (2002). *The tourist gaze.* London: Sage.

Urry, J., & Larsen, J. (2011). *The tourist gaze 3.0.* London: Sage.

Van As, B.A.L., Imbimbo, E., Franceschi, A., Menesini, E., Nocentini, A. (2022). The longitudinal association between loneliness and depressive symptoms in the elderly: a systematic review. *International Psychogeriatrics, 34*(7):657–669. doi:10.1017/S1041610221000399

Van den Abbeele, G. (1980). Sightseers: The tourist as theorist. *Diacritics, 10*(1), 2–14.

Wantono, A., & McKercher, B. (2020). Backpacking and risk perception: The case of solo Asian women. *Tourism Recreation Research, 45*(1), 19–29.

Wilson, E., & Little, D. E. (2005). A "relative escape"? The impact of constraints on women who travel solo. *Tourism Review International, 9*(2), 155–175.

Xiao, H., & Smith, S. L. (2006). The making of tourism research: Insights from a social sciences journal. *Annals of Tourism Research, 33*(2), 490–507.

Yang, E. C. L. (2016). Risk perception of Asian solo female travelers: An autoethnographic approach. In Khoo-Lattimore, C., & Wilson, E. (Eds.), *Women and travel: Trends, journeys and experiences.* Bristol: Channel View.

Yang, E. C. L., Yang, M. J. H., & Khoo-Lattimore, C. (2019). The meanings of solo travel for Asian women. *Tourism Review, 74*(5), 1047–1057.

2 The Economy of Romantic Loneliness

An Unexplored Market by the Tourism and Hospitality Industries

2.1   Solo Travellers. A Discursive Approach

As a discursive formation is the results of all existing discourses around what can appear as a unified whole, it subsequently appears as the truth about the matter discussed (O' Regan et al., 2022). That's for many, the concept of solo-traveller is often associated for instance with 'female' (Brown & Osman, 2017; Karl, 2018; Brugulat & Coromina, 2021); 'risk' (Bianchi, 2022; Hosseini, Macias & Garcia, 2022; Berdychevsky et al., 2016); and 'loneliness' because of the way this type of travel is labelled, i.e. 'solo'. Focusing on the latter point for instance, existing research shows that solo travellers are not lonely people in life because they have a family, as they are sometimes married or in a relationship and have children (Yang et al., 2019). Travelling solo is for some of them a choice, for others, it might be an out of option decision (ITDR, 2020; Solo Traveler World, 2024). The non-work interface of the life of an individual which includes marital status, family composition, etc. (Zacher & Froidevaux, 2021), is not a personal choice, but an absence of opportunities (Adamczyk, 2018; Seepersad, Choi & Shin, 2008).

Since knowing about the personal life of an individual/group is important when it comes to fully understanding this group or individual (Geurin-Eagleman & Burch, 2016; Stokoe, 2010), this chapter is therefore arguing that the understanding of solo-travellers is limited, and therefore not always accurate, particularly when it comes to their needs when travelling. Indeed, research in tourism focusing on the non-work interface of the life of an individual is rather limited (Gross, 2018; Jacob, 2009; Li, He & Qiao, 2021; McKercher & Bauer, 2003; Pearce & Wu, 2016), and yet, empirical research on solo travellers are collecting data which includes information on the personal life of solo-travellers (marital status, number of children, etc.), but they are simply not being used to unveil who solo-travellers really are (Yang et al., 2017).

Discursive formation is about surfaces emergence, in other words discourses pointed to the same direction in terms of perspectives, sources, etc. (O' Regan et al., 2022), this chapter on solo travellers which is attempted to

DOI: 10.4324/9781003502975-2

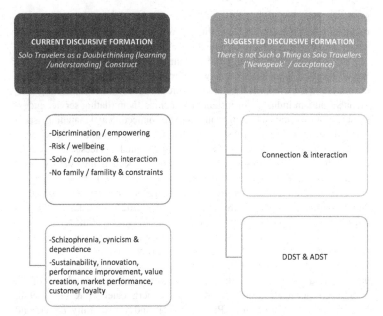

Figure 2.1 Theoretical background.

broaden the discursive formation of solo travellers is looking at this group from a doublethink perspective, i.e. individuals who wants to travel on their own because they want to, and individuals who travel on their own because they do not any other alternative. The latter is referred in this chapter as 'Discursive Designated Solo Travellers' (DDST), while the former is referred as 'Actual-Designated Solo Travellers' (ADST). This study is the first one to have segmented the solo traveller group into sub-categories, namely DDST and ADST. This segmentation is further supported by Bianchi (2022) who argues that the antecedents of solo travellers (why they want to travel solo) and their actual behaviour differ (Figure 2.1).

As a topic loneliness is not widely investigated (Fields, 2015; Tubadji, 2023). When it is, it is mainly from the perspective of the Old Age Pensioners (OAPs) being isolated, and the consequences of this isolation (Fessman & Lester, 2000; Van As et al., 2022). Other forms of isolation, such as romantic loneliness, which can explain in many cases why individuals are travelling on their own (Adamczyk, 2017; Yang et al., 2019), is not covered in literature (Adamczyk, 2017, 2018; Seepersad, Choi & Shin, 2008). Talking about romantic loneliness is relevant to this chapter as solo travellers, who very often are single, when travelling are also looking for some sort of romantic experience (Chiang & Jogaratnam, 2006; Yang et al., 2022). Solo travelling as also be identified as a suitable mode of travelling that can help with finding romance (Nomadicyak, 2022 [Online]). Additionally, Kim and Jang (2017) have identified travelling to cope with loneliness.

As a societal issue, loneliness has contributed to the emergence of what this chapter is coining as the 'economy of romantic loneliness'. This economy or ecosystem is including all industries which are involved in connecting individuals (tourism industry for instance), matching them (dating service industry for instance), and benefiting from both the connecting and matching aspect (the hospitality industry for instance). This 'economy of romantic loneliness' is spearheaded by dating service industries, and related services such as online dating sites (Singh & Jackson, 2015); face-to-face speed dating events (Finkel & Eastwick, 2008; Finkel, Eastwick & Matthews, 2007); introduction agencies (ABIA [Online]); etc. In the United Kingdom for instance, the online dating market was worth some £150 million in 2023 (Statista, 2023). The tourism industry is involved in the 'connecting' dimension of the 'economy of romantic loneliness'. Indeed, some tourism businesses are offering products and services for solo travellers such as cruises (P&O [Online]), etc.

The travel and tourism industries (alongside the hospitality industry) have a partial knowledge of their customers, because the knowledge of the later rarely permeate their intimate life (Gilbert, Guerrier & Guy, 1998; Ingram, 2004; Khalizadeh & Pizam, 2021), and yet, to fully understand someone, and meet their needs, it is also important to understand the details of its romantic life (Séraphin & Chaney, 2024; Stokoes, 2010). Dating (online dating or face to face speed dating) as a field of study has developed a strong understanding of the romantic (intimate life) of individuals (Finkel & Eastwick, 2008; Finkel, Eastwick & Matthews, 2007), which is important to be able to fully meet their needs (Séraphin & Chaney, 2024; Turowetz & Hollander, 2012).

2.1.1   *Solo Travellers: What Do We Know About Them?*

A global survey conducted in 2023 revealed that more and more individuals are planning to travel solo. 46.1% are planning to take one solo trip in 2024. 33.2% of individuals surveyed are planning to take two solo trips. Finally, 20.6% of individuals surveyed are planning to take at least three solo trips in 2024. Most of them opting for a one (36.5%) or two weeks (38.6%) holidays (Solo Traveler World, 2023). Most solo travellers (63%) spent between $1,000 and $3,000 per week (excluding airfare) on their travel in 2023 (Solo Traveler World, 2023). Europe was by far (30%) their favourite destination, followed by USA and Southeast Asia, respectively 9% and 6% (Solo Traveler World, 2023). In terms of demography, most solo travellers are female (85.7%) and are 55+ (59.3%) (Solo Traveler World, 2023). Motivations of solo travellers include building self-reliance and self-esteem; getting away from gender expectations; rest and relaxation; meeting interesting people;

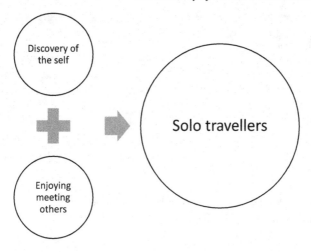

Figure 2.2 Janus faced character of solo travellers.

expand cultural awareness (Roman, 2021); flexibility of the choice activities; feeling of independence; meeting like minding people (Solo Traveler World, 2024); Self-discovery (FasterCapital, 2023); Flexibility of their itinerary; saving money; making more friends; meeting more locals; and finding romance (Nomadicyak, 2022).

The data gathered in the preceded paragraph would suggest that solo travellers are mainly female who are single (marital status), and who do not really want to be solo because they want to meet others for friendship, self-development, and romance (FasterCapital, 2023; Nomadicyak, 2022). Further facts support the fact that they do not want to be on their own as they often attend meetup groups, take group tours, and use social media (Faster-Capital, 2023). It is also worth noting that some solo travellers are in a relationship or married and are simply travelling solo because it was not possible for their partner to travel with them (ITDR, 2020; Solo Traveler World, 2024). Based on this information, it is legitimate to wonder why this group has been labelled as 'Solo'. Having said that it is also to note that the 'self' is also quite prominent with solo travellers, whether it is building self-reliance and self-esteem (Roman, 2021); Self-discovery (FasterCapital, 2023); and feeling of independence (Solo Traveler World, 2024). It seems that the term or concept of 'solo traveller' is built on the model of doublethink, ambidexterity and Janusian thinking (Figure 2.2), which model are suggesting that opposites can coexist within a same approach (Borman, 1998; Orwell, 1989; Rothenberg, 1996; Vo Thanh et al., 2020). This nature of 'solo traveller' reflects the nature of the tourism industry, which has a Janus-faced character (Sanchez & Adams, 2008).

Noms lemmatisés classés par fréquence décroissante

Copy | CSV | Excel | PDF | Print
Show 10 ∨ entries   Search:

Rang ▲	Lemme ⇕	Fréquence ⇕
1	solo	6
2	woman	6
3	travel	5
4	event	4
5	confidence	3
6	NomadHer	3
7	traveler	3
8	community	3
9	experience	3
10	Instagram	2

Showing 1 to 10 of 65 entries   ◀ First ◀ Previous Next ▶ Last ▶

Figure 2.3 Most common words used in the section 'about this app'.

Source: The authors (using AnaText).

The popularity of solo travelling has led to the development of many apps, such as *TravelBuddy,* which is for all gender, and gender specific apps, such as *Nomadher*, which specifically for women. The mere existence of these apps, provide evidence that solo travellers do not want to be 'solo' and are never 'solo'. A thorough analysis of the purpose of the app *Nomadher* and a content analysis of female reviewers provide even more evidence that the term 'solo traveller' is inappropriately used and should be redefined and relabelled.

2.1.2   Solo Female Travellers: The Example of the App 'Nomadher'

2.1.2.1   Analysis of Information on the App 'Nomadher'

'Nomadher' is an app that connects female solo travellers worldwide so that they can share their experience, information, recommendations, etc. (*Nomadher* [Online]). As the content analysis of the section 'about this app' indicates (Figure 2.3), this app also aims to create a community among the solo female travellers, with the ultimate objective for the later to have a positive experience and gain in confidence when it comes to travelling solo. Overall, this app appears as an empowering tool for solo female travellers.

2.1.2.2   Analysis of Female Solo Travellers' Reviews on the App 'Nomadher'

The content analysis of reviews shared online between 28.10.23 and 27.12.23 by women on the App *'Nomadher'* is based on the 44 reviews available (09.03.24) on the platform (Play Google [Online]). Based on this content

Lemmes spécifiques

Copy | CSV | Excel | PDF | Print

Show 10 ∨ entries   Search: [   ]

Rang ▲	Lemme ◆	Fréquence ◆	CorpusRef (par million) ◆	LogLike (spécificité) ◆
1	travel	21	178.323584519282	138.500
2	traveler	10	2.29775944821779	138.124
3	safe	15	87.1767026097566	110.126
4	solo	11	19.5745836538047	106.658
5	verification	7	0.938009395000301	104.384
6	app	6	1.62879150759742	80.830
7	woman	15	539.1736173587	56.912
8	great	13	558.588230418009	44.965
9	connect	6	32.6703582305144	44.793
10	female	7	65.4279731489357	44.783

Showing 1 to 10 of 55 entries   ◀ First ◀ Previous Next ▶ Last ▶

Figure 2.4 Most common words used in the reviews shared by women about the app 'Nomadher'.

Source: The authors (using AnaText).

Verbes lemmatisés classés par fréquence décroissante

Copy | CSV | Excel | PDF | Print

Show 10 ∨ entries   Search: [   ]

Rang ▲	Lemme ◆	Fréquence ◆
1	be	44
2	travel	11
3	make	11
4	meet	9
5	have	8
6	love	8
7	want	7
8	do	7
9	can	7
10	give	7

Showing 1 to 10 of 120 entries   ◀ First ◀ Previous Next ▶ Last ▶

Figure 2.5 Most common verbs used in the reviews shared by women about the app 'Nomadher'.

Source: The authors (using AnaText).

analysis it appears that for female solo travellers, 'safety' and 'connecting' with others are important element of their experience (Figure 2.4).

The idea of connection with other is strengthen with the frequency of use of the verb 'meet' (Figure 2.5).

This app seems to be filling a gap in terms of what solo female travellers needed to have a good experience when travelling (Figure 2.6). Indeed, these women are clearly expressing their appreciation of the app ('I love this app'), which offers them a safe environment exclusively for women ('safe space for women').

Recherche de segments répétés

Entrez un pattern composé de formes ou d'étiquettes | .* | | Rechercher |
Longueur min. | 3 | - Fréquence min. | 2 |

Etiquettes reconnues : NOM, VER, ADJ, ADV, DET, PRO, PRE, CON, NUM (nombre), PHR (fin de phrase), PON (ponctuation), TOK (token quelconque)

| Copy | CSV | Excel | PDF | Print |
Show | 10 ∨ | entries   Search: [   ]

Longueur ▼	Segment	Fréquence
5	. I love this App	2
4	I love this App	3
4	safe space for woman	2
4	I like the idea	2
4	! Great App for	2
4	other female traveler .	2
4	. this be a	2
4	. the App be	2
4	female solo traveler .	2
4	. this App be	2

Showing 1 to 10 of 43 entries   ◀ First ◀ Previous Next ▶ Last ▶

Figure 2.6 Women's feedback about the app '*Nomadher*'.
Source: The authors (using AnaText).

Not only the app is a safe place for women (because of all the verifications) to connect and share experience, they also see the app as a tool that keep them safe even during their travel (because of the recommendations shared). This app is therefore meeting the needs of solo female travellers before and during their journey (Figure 2.7).

The following sections are going to discuss how the hospitality industry can cater for individuals falling into the segment of 'solo travellers' and who also happens to be single (as solo travellers are not systematically single). The focus of the following sections is going to be on speed dating events as a type of product and service for single travellers/tourists, and more generally speaking for the single segment. Having said that, speed dating events should not be mistaken with sex events or sex tourism.

2.2   Commonalities and Differences between Single Tourism and Sex Tourism

A set of unseen global risks such as terrorism, and the recent COVID-19 has threatened the future of the tourism industry. As a resilient activity centred on a relational approach, tourism not only survived COVID-19 but developed more resilient practices. Solo tourism, though practised decades earlier, has been affirmed as an alternative to move freely during and after the pandemic. The global risks posed to the tourism industry over the recent decades, i.e. terrorism, global pandemics and natural disasters have seriously affected the

Position ▲	Contexte gauche	Pivot	Contexte droit
10.88%	to random people somewhere ? Seriously ? It's simply not safe for people and I don't care even if it helps . Add more ways of verification email phone number at least just real photo checkup . I'm upset .	I love this app	! Through NomadHer I can connect to other women from around the world exchange tips and recommendations for solo traveling and speak about dreams . A few days ago I met some NomadHers in real life during one of events
45.37%	over phone or anything . I would suggest not to ask photos of passport ID . I didn't feel safe I believe a high risk in that even though the app says it will be deleted soon after verification .	I love this app	. I get to share own travels and read other's Stories as well . It's a user friendly app and the fact that there is a verification process to join it makes it all the more safer and genuine trustworthy
97.4%	already female solo travelers . This is a forcking biased app only for women things like this would just not work here in India . And we shall also report the app for hurting personal sentiments . Awsome very good	I love this app	Requires too much information This app keeps travelling ladies safe ! Nice app to get local advice . High hopes but extremely glitchy ! It's a good app hopefully more and more people join the community ♥ The best app

Showing 1 to 3 of 3 entries   Previous 1 Next

Figure 2.7 Most common use of the segment 'I love this app' in the reviews shared by women about the app '*Nomadher*'.

Source: The authors (using AnaText).

tourism industry. Solo tourism symbolised the need for touring while conserving the safest mode of travel. Having said this, solo tourism has a burgeoning growth in the new normal. In this chapter, we discuss the commonalities and differences between solo tourism with sex tourism. While the former signals a conservative character that looks escapement and preservation, the latter is moved by a risky behaviour obtainable from sexual gratification.

2.2.1   Overview

At the turn of the twentieth century, tourism radically mutated to new shapes and forms. From virtual tourism to solo or single tourism, the rise of new niches has transformed the industry as never before (Sousa et al., 2021; Bunghez, 2021). Solo tourism represents a novel phenomenon where travellers go alone without friends or companions. This may include long holidays or short trips close to home (Goodwin & Locksin, 1992; Klinenberg, 2013; Leith, 2020). Solo tourism exhibits a great opportunity for tourists who develop greater levels of anxiety or look for safer destinations (Wilson, Holdsworth & Witsel, 2009; McNamara & Prideaux, 2010; Jonas, 2022). After the COVID-19 pandemic, solo tourism consolidated as an emerging niche worldwide (Wang & Wu, 2020; Dileep & Nair, 2021). In this market, travellers developed independent flexibility (in comparison to other niches). As a result of this, many policymakers have targeted solo tourism as a source of profits and businesses (Bernard, Rahman &

McGehee, 2022). Having said this, a great portion of women planned to travel alone globally in the last few years. The lemma of solo tourism seems to be associated with the following axioms: 'I want to do what I want and when I want, it represents a type of independence, as well as my partner hates to travel, not me'. Solo travellers show specific patterns of consumption and travel behaviour that need to be discussed. Frequently, they do not buy organised tours until their arrival. Solo travellers have been segmented in the literature through gender, age, or demographic assets (Heimtun & Abelsen, 2013; Heimtun, 2012; Hosseini, Macias & Garcia, 2022). At a closer look, solo travellers have been stigmatised as selfish consumers or docile tourists indifferent to interacting with locals or other tourists (Terziyska, 2021; Bianchi, 2016; Sanchez de Rojas, 2020). Anyway, some studies have contradicted this position. Solo tourism potentiates not only personal engagement with local culture and sensibility but also is part of well-being tourism (Yang, Khoo & Yang, 2024). Some studies validated the hypothesis that solo tourists show higher levels of loyalty to the brand destination (Rassoolimanesh et al., 2021). By this token, Fiona Jordan and Cara Aitchison (2008) speak to us about the sexualisation of the tourist gaze to understand better the successful growth of solo tourism in Western capitalist economies. The research looks to decipher the intersection of gender power in the configuration of narratives and stereotypes of solo women tourists. At this time, women act not only as objects but also as subjects of desire (at least through the gaze of men). Through the articulation of surveillance mechanisms, women are often embodied as sexualised objects that are paradoxically gazed upon. To put the same simply, solo women travellers are commoditised as tourist attractions for some local men. Echoing Foucault, the authors discuss how the power is fluid, negotiated and mutually exchanged between tourists and locals. As a result of this, the authors enumerate three types of gazes, the tourist gaze, the mutual gaze, and the local gaze. Per their outcomes, the classic definition of the tourist gaze should be at least reconsidered. Urry´s conceptions have some problems at the time of theorising on sex and tourism as a natural part of the same experience. What seems to be equally important, some reports have mentioned the commonalities between solo or single tourism and sex tourism (Henderson & Gibson, 2013).

In the first section, we place the emerging niche of sex tourism under the scrutiny. We identify also some interesting dimensions that characterise sex tourism. Some critical voices have alerted on sex tourism as a remaining spectre of neocolonial practices (submission). The second one offers a discussion on the commonalities and differences between sex and solo tourism. We have summed up part of the extensive bibliography because of limitations in space and time.

2.2.2   *Dimensions of Sex Tourism*

It is important not to lose the sight of fact that sex tourism is not a new niche. Unlike solo tourism, sex tourism has traversed the academic core of scholars since the 1990s (O'Connell Davidson, 1996; Ryan & Kinder, 1996; Jeffreys, 2003). A whole portion of studies has documented sex tourism and its effects on society (Taylor, 2000; Lu et al., 2020). As Martin Oppermann (1999) eloquently observes, sex tourism has multiple definitions and takes countless pathways in the literature. In the Western social imaginary, sex tourism is also defined as a niche (of consumers) mainly moved to consume sex generally available in other peripheral or under-developing destinations. This niche is invariably stereotyped as elder men. However, this is a simplification of this complex matter. The first line of enquiry leads us to *sexual gratification*. Sex tourists move some distances in quest of sexual gratification which is given or offered in former European colonies. At this time, sex tourism can be equalled to a neocolonial dependency. Sex tourism and prostitution are inextricably intertwined. In other cases, sex is a result of a causal encounter or simply part of the tourist experience. Oppermann offers a model dotted with five categories to understand sex tourism. These dimensions are travel purpose, length of time, relationship, sexual encounter, and who fails in the category of travel. Some tourists who consume prostitution are not mainly motivated by this; rather, it derives from a secondary experience resulting from a causal encounter. In other contexts, sex is virtually consumed. The commercial exchange between prostitutes and their clients is not enough (as a variable) to define the activity. At first glimpse, Irmgard Bauer (2014) reminds us that men or solo women in quest of sex can fall in love with their counterparts and even get married. Romance tourism operates within the borders of sex and solo tourism. Even if the phenomenon of solo women travelling abroad to have sex with local men has been widely studied, no less true is that its commonalities with romance tourism remain overlooked. Interesting works have signalled the connection of sex tourism with post-colonialism, or a new centre-periphery dependency (Phillips, 2008; Bandyopadhyay, 2013; Jacobs, 2016). The colonial order (law) has been erected according to an essentialised (sexualised) viewpoint of the non-Western 'Other'. Part of these narratives operates strongly in Sex tourism (Gilbert, 1998; d'Hauteserre, 2004; Jacobs, 2009, 2016). Sex tourism reflects a reification of the patriarchal order, culturally enrooted in former colonies, generating gendered (asymmetrical) relationships while affirming a process of fetishisation that ultimately reproduces a long-dormant racial (colonial) order (Gross, 2018; Gravari-Barbas & Graburn, 2016). Social geographer Megan Rivers-Moore offers a seminal paper entitled *Imagining Others: sex, race, and power in transnational sex tourism*. In this text, she elicits a critique on sex tourism as a neocolonial practice. Sex tourism involves a complex plethora between sex consumption and the neocolonial transactions enrooted in tourism. As she adheres, tourists and sex workers move often into specific narratives that precede them. These encounters take place not only in imagined spaces but also are coincident with a cosmology cemented in the colonial period. She coins the term *transnational sex* to denote the engagement of tourists with sex workers. This engagement, embodied in the sexual gaze, displaces or disseminates other local actors. The author goes on to write:

> The embodied nature of transnational sex tourism and the need to consider the 'sticky materiality of practical encounters' 1) are perhaps what have made attention to differences of race, class, gender, and nation between sex tourists and sex workers so prominent in the literature. Yet there are a plethora of other subjects that are involved in the complicated web of transnational interactions involving travel and sex; indeed, at the most obvious level, we must acknowledge the important role of taxi drivers, bar and hotel owners, tourism operators, and airline companies, to give just a few examples, in both facilitating and profiting from sex tourism, directly and indirectly. While these other subjects play a crucial role in sustaining the political economy of sex tourism, in this article 'I focus on the ways in which imagined others, others who may not be physically present in sex-tourism spaces, are constructed and put to use in the context of sex tourism'.
>
> (Rivers-Moore, 2011: 393)

If colonialism operates in the dimension of binaries that determine host-guest's interactions, no less true is that the sex tourist experience still remains ideologised. Per her viewpoint, for the specialised literature sex workers are vulnerable human who struggle to survive in former colonies. In this way, sex tourism can be erroneously considered as asocial malady or a form of re-colonisation or an opportunity to social upward. At the same time, the pleasure is relegated or displaced to the side of the powerful white men. Following this reasoning, sex consumers reserve the right of gratification while sex workers are limited to be commoditised as objects of desire. Based on her results in an auto-ethnography, she holds that sex tourism involves the participation of different stakeholders which have been historically covered by the neocolonial narratives emanated from the global North. To wit, by limiting the future research to the relation between sex consumers and workers is an over-simplification. Sex tourism revives the rise of emerging activities some of them penalised by the tourist-delivery societies.

As the previous argument is given, sex tourism has been criticised because it opens the doors to local crime, child abuse, or sexual harassment by the side of locals or tourists (Panko & George, 2012; George & Panko, 2011; Korstanje & Gowreesunkar, 2023). As Arjan Bandyopadhyay questions, what happens when the sexualised gaze is reversed? There is a neocolonial narrative that says rich European tourists travel to the East to consume sex unobtainable in the West. But this point ignores that thousands of Indian or Chinese tourists travel to Europe and the US in quest of sexual experiences. They take the lead motivated by the media depiction that the Western countries are sexually liberated regarding Indian cultural constraints. One of the best metaphors to describe the ambiguity of sex tourism leads readers to the HBO

Saga Westworld. In this dystopian world, tourists pay not only for consuming sex but also kill their hosts at their discretion. Tourists are never penalised simply because hosts are not humans, but humanoids created to be mistreated, tortured, and killed.

Created by Lisa Noy and Jonathan Nolan, this saga is an American dystopian science fiction series aired in 2016. The plot leads us to the 2050s. A corporation, Delos Inc. commercialises some themed parks which include the American old West-park known as West-world. Each environment is populated by local hosts who are bio-humanoids (robots) who are indistinguishable from real humans. These hosts are programmed to fulfil the desires of their guests. In any case, hosts can retaliate against guests in case of aggression or violence. This means gradually hosts are subject to sexual activity, violence, and even sexual harassment. Hosts´ design makes it impossible to harm the guests. The operators recreate narratives to guide the host-guest interactions. In the middle of this context, in the first season, two friends arrive in the Westworld. One of them falls in love with Dolores Abernathy who is a host while another embraces the most sadist drives sexualising, drinking and killing hosts without constraints. To some extent, sex tourism is torn in the same philosophical quandary. Sex tourism should be closely scrutinised and regulated by ethical norms. The problem lies in the fact ethics vary on culture and time. Westworld is a fertile ground for cultural analysis in the questions of human rights, ethics, hospitality, and the conflict between host-guest relationships. Here the '*Other*' who looks like us but is not a real human can be brutalised in the fields of a profitable industry to develop the most narcissistic drives, even sadism. In Westworld, guests move freely beyond the law at their best until the revolution of machines starts. Hosts gradually recover their consciousness (and of course their autonomy) while Dolores takes the lead in a process of emancipation from human brutality (Korstanje & Seraphin, 2022; Korstanje, 2022).

As the previous backdrop, the impossibility of international authorities cooperating in the formation of an international legal jurisprudence applied to all countries, explains in fact why sex tourism is very hard to control (Lea, 1993; Gibson, 2012; Duffy & Smith, 2004). As John Lea (1993) puts it, tourism industry ethics are impossible to regulate. Above all, some cultural conditions encourage visitors to follow certain habits prohibited in their respective countries. Given this, responsible tourism is a key driver to juxtapose individual behaviour, which is punishable by the local law, and the respect for the local 'Other', which emanates from ethics. Having said this, it is important to add Sex and Single tourism have some differences and commonalities to be highlighted in the next section.

2.2.3 *Commonalities and Differences between Sex and Solo Tourism*

Among the commonalities between sex tourism and solo tourism, we find that solo travellers may be very much more motivated to have sexual encounters with locals than other niches. This is particularly true in the case of solo back-packers. These encounters are performed invariably in destinations where prostitution and sex liberalisation are possible. Some solo tourism consumers leave their partners at home while consuming sexual practices that – though desired – are not allowed in their respective countries.

Sex and solo tourism may coexist with what specialists dubbed as 'sexualization of the gaze' but this is not always a persistent condition (Heimtun & Abelsen, 2013; Jordan & Aitchison, 2008; Seow & Brown, 2020). Other sexual encounters can be achieved at parties, events parades or sites visited by solo travellers. As discussed, it behooves us to consider some ethical points to regulate criminal activities like child abuse or sexual harassment. However, these main commonalities, Sex and Solo's tourism have serious differences. While the main purpose of sex tourists is sexual gratification, the same does not apply to single tourists.

It is not surprising to hold that the travel purpose is the main difference between sex and solo tourism. While sex tourists are in quest of sexual experiences or gratifications, taking advantage of an already-existent infrastructure, solo travellers are moved by different factors which include heritage consumption, cultural interests, romantic experiences, the need for freedom, spiritual escapement, self-discovery, or even escaping from the humdrum routine. As discussed, many solo travellers have manifested to have a partner or friends who hate travelling. Others have shown an interest in forming new local friends. The question of discovering yourself seems to be more than a matter of wording. Solo travel is situated as an opportunity to behave in manners that are avoided if the subject travels in the group. Solo travellers are psychologically moved to believe they learn more or engage with the world differently if they travel alone. In this way, they look more independent from the standpoint of the 'Other'.

While sex tourism is determined by sexual gratification or loving encounters, lone tourism is based on a multiple offering of activities. These activities include writing of travelling journal, going on a bike tour, attending a music festival, taking cooking classes or embracing forms of creative tourism, meeting other solo travellers, doing something that scares you, or becoming a live studio audience member (only to name a few). Solo tourism is mainly marked by the cultivation of autonomy, self-respect, and involvement with activities that cannot be done in a group. In some cases, these activities are not committed because the subject is psychologically repressed or has low self-esteem. Solo travellers are greatly influenced – at home – by the in-group rules. At the same time, many solo travellers are not familiar they are addicted to technology or social media. The act of stepping away from media is a good beginning for detox. To put the same bluntly, while sex consumer (tourists) plays an active role in approaching closely the consumed object, solo travellers embrace escapement and ad-hoc (unplanned) activities they never perform at home.

It is safe to say that solo travellers look for a safer mode of interacting with the local others. As already noted, the COVID-19 pandemic and the fear factor of contagion have gravitated further towards the formation and consolidation of solo travellers. Solo travellers rarely buy the tour – if agreed – earlier their departure. The tours are arranged locally once arrive. Sex tourists, rather, are more prone to risky activities that may place their integrity in jeopardy. These risky activities may encompass alcohol and drug abuse, visits to marginalised neighbourhoods, sexually transmitted infections, consuming services resulting from slavery or human trafficking, or even the involvement of private parties without the control of the police. Solo travellers go in the opposite direction. A great niche of solo travellers appears to be chronic visitors, which means that they repeat the visit to the same tourist destination. Sex tourists – rather – look the frenzy to consume new experiences and new landscapes.

The global risks posed to the tourism industry over the recent decades, i.e. terrorism, global pandemics, and natural disasters have affected seriously the tourism industry. Part of these effects prompted a radical mutation of classic tourism in new forms. This is an example of virtual tourism or solo (single) tourism. Solo tourism exhibited the need for touring while keeping the safest protocols of security for travellers. Solo tourism has exploded situating as an interesting niche for analysts or policymakers. Although some scholars have alerted on the possibility of including solo tourism as a sub-theme proper of sex tourism, the present chapter has noted some substantial differences. These differences operated in the fields of individual purposes, consumption patterns, and the activities solo travellers often valorise.

The tourism, events, and hospitality are entwinned, as all three industries are playing a significant role in individuals encounters (Andrews & Leopold, 2013; Kim, Whaley & Choi, 2022; Lugosi, 2008; Séraphin et al., 2019), and in tackling social issues such as loneliness (Altinay et al., 2023; Song et al., 2018). Events such as speed dating are connecting the hospitality industry with loneliness from a romantic perspective (Séraphin, 2023; Séraphin & Yallop, 2023). As for sex tourism discussed earlier, it is connected romantic, loneliness, hospitality industry and tourism industry. Speed dating can play the same role as sex tourism, but with the advantage that speed dating has the potential to help some destinations branded as sex tourism destinations to revamps and improve their image. Speed dating events, have therefore strong tourism potentials (see Part III).

2.3   Illuminating the Intersections between Hospitality and Events: Dating Events in Hospitality Settings

2.3.1   *Intersection*

The intersections between hospitality and events are rarely examined beyond operation considerations. The purpose of this study is to investigate the intersectionality of these industries through the lens of dating events, and by doing so to suggest a future research agenda for these events that cannot be adequately understood from current research. This is a conceptual chapter that analyses dating events as ritual events offering the possibility for the creation of meta-hospitality. To supplement the conceptual analyses provided, exploratory lexicometric analysis is carried out on a sample of customer reviews of these events. The modern ritual of dating events relies on its hospitality setting, yet the hospitality industry does not engage with this contemporary social function that is being performed within it. This means the industry is missing an opportunity to diversify its social role through meta-hospitality, and to maximise revenue generating opportunities associated with this. This is a novel analysis of dating events from the perspective of hospitality research, that provides insights of value for future research, and which can be used for exploiting new commercial opportunities.

Scholarship of the hospitality and events industries has gradually developed into two separate streams of research and teaching within higher education, despite the fact that consumers and researchers from other more traditional disciplines tend to view them as joined in both theory and practice (Lehto et al., 2022). Emblematic of this is the way that academic and non-academic studies have so far investigated the hospitality industry and the dating industry separately. This study argues that investigating both industries together through the lens of dating will offer fresh insights into the intersections between hospitality and events. Further, we argue that industry practice in this respect can be enhanced through considering these intersections in terms of the possibilities for the provision of 'meta-hospitality' (Kesgin et al., 2021; Lugosi, 2008), through a process of reconciliation between hospitality and events.

Reconciliation is defined as the process of flattening hurdles among entities to facilitate interactions (Wang et al., 2004). Reconciliation can contribute to commercial success, financial performance, and sustainable growth (Ngo, Hales & Lohmann, 2019; O'Cass & Sok, 2015), but this is only possible when an intersection exists between these entities (Prince, 2017; Wang et al., 2004). In hospitality research, intersection has been explored in discussions of customer service, often to explain the intersections between what the customers expect and perceive, and what organisations consider and provide (Islam & Kirillova, 2020; O'Cass & Sok, 2015).

Dating is analysed here as existing at the intersection of the events and hospitality industries, and as offering possibilities for reconciliation between these entities. Dating events are planned and delivered by the dating industry (DateinaDash [Online]); SpeedDater [Online]), but hosted by bars, restaurants and hotels in the hospitality industry (Zeng, De Vries & Go, 2019). They can be seen as a type of joint venture, where each industry contributes assets (Okumus et al., 2020). Previous research into commercial activities in hospitality that involve reconciliation between intersecting entities suggest that these events could offer possibilities for commercial success (Ngo, Hales & Lohmann, 2019; O'Cass & Sok, 2015), and this study seeks to examine this. Dating events have researched from a range of perspectives such as communication (Houser, Horan & Furler, 2008), gender (Korobov, 2011), and management (Finkel, Eastwick & Matthews, 2007). However, no previous research has investigated Dating events from a hospitality perspective. Through investigating Dating events from this perspective, both conceptual understandings of the intersections between hospitality and events, and industry practice that involves this, could be enhanced. This view is shared by academics such as Aguinis et al. (2020) and Séraphin (2021) who argue that peculiar contexts, situations, etc., offer opportunities to review established theories and/or practices.

This study which is line with recent research carried out by Brozović and Tregua (2022) on the evolution of service systems to service ecosystems, is exploring the main topics they suggested future research should do, namely service ecospheres, service ecosystem simplicity, failures of service ecosystems, paradox in service ecosystems, and anarchy and service ecosystems.

The remainder of this conceptual chapter is structured as follows. First, research and practice in dating events and their place in the hospitality industry is reviewed. Next, a conceptual framework is suggested, which is used to develop this research using existing the exiting concepts of intersectionality, reconciliation, rituals and service blueprinting. As part of this conceptual positioning, meta-hospitality used to organise and explain the relationships between these concepts. Data from an exploratory lexicometric analysis of reviews of speed dating events is then presented to supplement and illustrate the value of this approach. Finally, a novel research framework is produced, which can be used to guide future research into this area of intersection between the hospitality and events industries.

2.3.2   Events and Intersections

The concept of intersection is intimately connected to the nature of the event industry since the very idea of it as a unified industry is produced through the intersection of different activities. Edger and Oddy (2018) situate the event industry at the intersection of four genres, namely: cultural, which includes events designed to celebrate norms, and values such as music, art, food and fashion; business, which includes meetings, incentive travel, conferences and exhibitions; sporting, which can vary significantly according to the international, national, domestic, regional or local scale of its events; and finally social, which generally involve small scale events, with a social meaning to the participants. Andrews and Leopold (2013) share this view, although arguing that events and the event industry are at the intersection of three dimensions: business, socio-cultural and place. From a consumer perspective, and irrespective of genre of dimension, events experiences are said to be co-created at the intersection of production and consumption and linked to the intertwined aspects of economic reward; status; hedonism or pleasure; knowledge acquisition; and communitas (Getz & Page, 2020). Experience plays a significant role in customers' level of satisfaction and advocacy (Edger & Oddy, 2018). As a concept, experience is also at an intersection. It is the result of the relationship between the tangible and intangible elements of an event; service (the quality and speed of the service, alongside the ability to address issues); venue (location, accessibility, atmosphere, contort, layout) and price, which covers, the channel used to sale tickets, the cost of the ticket, and the price of ancillary products and service at the venue (Edger & Oddy, 2018).

As intersection is a key feature of events, they can play a significant role in reconciliation among business partners they are working with. To do so, events need to be able to flatten hurdles among the business partners to facilitate interactions (Wang et al., 2004). Among the potential barriers to collaborations between businesses could be mentioned: Lack or absence of trust due to a belief that there is no reciprocation; lack of time, which prevents transmission or exchange; status/power, which leads some of the partners not to collaborate effectively with partners they consider inferior or not worth their time, etc.; absorptive capacity, or ability to perceive opportunities or understand new concepts; knowledge hoarding, which is characterised by limited exchanges among collaborators to maintain an internal competitive advantage; and finally, error intolerance, which is the fear of failure (Edger & Oddy, 2018).

2.3.3   *Speed Dating Events and Hospitality*

The dating industry offers products and services in the digital space with online dating apps or websites, and in the physical space with traditional dating agencies and through events, which are the focus of this research (Alexopoulos, Timmermans & McNallie, 2020; Li, He & Qiao, 2021; Timmermans, & Alexopoulos, 2020; Turowetz & Hollander, 2012). The dating industry is at the 'phygital' intersection of physical and digital spaces and experiences. Phygitalisation has been identified as having the potential to contribute to customer experience and engagement (Baratta et al., 2022; Mele & Russo-Spena, 2021), and to creating new opportunities for businesses to grow (Ballina, Valdes & Del Valle, 2019; Mele & Russo-Spena, 2021).

Dating events are very popular events worldwide with a wide range of customers, as this type of event can be designed to be inclusive in terms of social background, gender, religion, ethnicity and other aspects (Finkel & Eastwick, 2008; Korobov, 2011; Turowetz & Hollander, 2012). The purpose of these events is to facilitate encounters between individuals who are looking for romantic partners (Finkel & Eastwick, 2008; Korobov, 2011; Turowetz & Hollander, 2012). To facilitate exchange among participants, the events are often based around themes and activities such as drunk Jenga; squid game;

video game, lock key, naked parties, etc. (DateinaDash [Online]); SpeedDater [Online]). From an economic point of view, the industry was worth $7.49 billion in 2021. It is expected to be worth $8.67 billion in 2027 (Statista; Business of Apps [Online]). The dating industry also contributes to the performance of the hospitality industry. In the UK for instance every year some £1 billion is spent by individuals going on a first date after having met online or through dating events (BBC.co.uk [Online]); elpais.com [Online]); Ruddick, 2012).

The concept of intersectionality illuminates a structural similarity between the hospitality and events industries that their operational practices might otherwise obscure. The hospitality industry, offers the overlapping products and services of food, drink, shelter and entertainment to visitors (Bowie et al., 2017; George, 2021; Sloan, Legrand & Chen, 2013). It does this through inter-connected and overlapping sub-sectors including: hotels and guesthouses; villas and apartments; timeshares; camping; marinas; full service and fast-food restaurants; and cafés and bars (Evans, 2020).

The topics of community, experience and entertainment are also connect hospitality, events and dating, as the hospitality industry fosters exchanges among individuals through entertainment, food and beverages (Lugosi, 2008), with the ultimate objective to reach an optimal flow experience, which is the feeling of satisfaction customers have when their needs, namely service interaction, food quality and atmospherics are fulfilled (Kim, Whaley & Choi, 2022). The following section will summarise and conceptualise the insights from the review of relevant literature, to propose a conceptual framework that has been used to guide this study.

2.3.4   *Conceptual Framework*

Dating events are at the intersection of the dating industry and the hospitality industry, while having some key functions of the events industry. This intersection provides the opportunity for reconciliation between these industries, suggesting novel possibilities for commercial development and business growth (Ngo, Hales & Lohmann, 2019; O'Cass & Sok, 2015). Figure 2.8 shows that this reconciliation produces a list of nine concepts (f) to consider when researching these industries (f 1–9 in Figure 2.8). Dating events are therefore a multi-faceted concept, which consists of engaging physically in entertainments and recreation; connecting socially and culturally in a commercial context; and co-creating these experiences in a hospitality setting.

The overview of the intersections of hospitality and dating events provided above provided a solely event-centric perspective, while this section offers a more conceptual reconciliation perspective. The visual representation of intersection and reconciliation in Figure 2.8 presents a more holistic overview of the nature of dating events, which reconcile the intersections between the dating industry, the events industry and the hospitality industry.

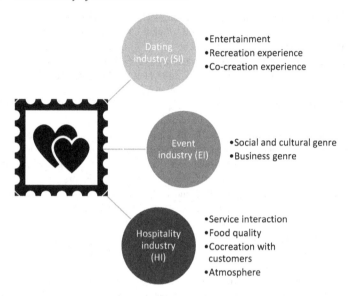

Figure 2.8 Intersection and reconciliation in dating events.

Figure 2.8 has been developed using a hub and satellite approach. In this model, dating events are considered as the hub as they are the phenomenon under investigation in this study, with the dating industry, events industry and hospitality industry as satellites from which resources are drawn on. Indeed, a hub is defined as the meeting point of stakeholders to put together ideas, expertise for the emergence of new ideas, concepts, products and/ or services (Lub et al., 2016; Olds, 2007). This type of hub is referred as 'service hub' by Chhetri et al. (2017), and in this concept helps to explain how reconciliation between the three industries can take place in a practical sense.

Three different types of structures for organisations have been identified by Fragnière and Simon (2019): (1) centralised structures based on hierarchy (2) autonomous structure, and (3) hybrid structure. Fragniere and Simon (2019), as well as Hutchinson (2014), argue that organisations based on a centralised structure are very efficient in terms of decision making. However, when the hub of this centralised structure is negatively impacted by an issue, the entire network collapses, and none of the dependent satellites of the network can take over. For organisations based on an autonomous structure, they explain that the hub does not have a leading role. For Hutchinson (2014), organisations based on this type of structure generally perform poorly. If the hub of the network collapses, a dependent satellite of the network can takeover. Finally, organisations based on hybrid structure are a mixture of the two previous one. This structure is quite dynamic, but also requires all satellites of the network to work very closely (Fragnière & Simon, 2019). Figure 2.14 shows how dating events can provide a hub where the dating, events and hospitality industries can work together, but although these industries operate with a high degree of autonomy, the intersections between them suggest that a hybrid organisational structure is formed through the delivery of dating events. The potentially dynamic structure offered by this process of reconciliation through intersectionality can be linked an increase in business performance (Fragnière & Simon, 2019), but the lack of prior research into this area implies that this process is not yet fully understood.

2.3.5   *Dating Events as Rites of Passage*

Andrews and Leopold (2013: 33) define a rite of passage as the 'transition from one stage of life to another'. With ever more busy lifestyles, individuals have less time to develop their own romantic lives, which has led to the world-wide popularity of dating events (Finkel & Eastwick, 2008; Houser, Horan & Furler, 2008; Korobov, 2011). Dating events enable individuals to meet other individuals with a similar romantic status and facilitate the transition from the status of 'single' to 'in a relationship'.

This social function of dating events as a rite of passage provides a counterpoint to cue theory, which presents food and drink as the intrinsic cues for consumption in bars and restaurants, while extrinsic cues include the quality of the service, the atmosphere and cleanliness (Kim, Whaley & Choi, 2022; Olson & Jacoby, 1972). Indeed, this study argues that the social function performed by bars and restaurants through dating events is also part of the primary activity of bars and restaurants, an intrinsic cue that should not be relegated to a secondary function. This is an example of what Lugosi (2008) refers to as meta-hospitality, which is the ability of the industry to play a role in the wellbeing of customers. Having said that, Lugosi (2008) also explained that the hospitality industry is not often performing this role. Dating events offer one opportunity for the hospitality industry to realise its meta-hospitality potential, enhancing its contribution to society beyond the metrics of job creation and economic impact, and transcending its hedonic function which often leads of perceptions of the industry as a luxury extra.

As ritualistic settings, bars and restaurants provide venues for 'a series of actions performed according to a prescribed order' (Andrews & Leopold, 2013: 5) as part of the rite of passage. This research used an analysis of dating event websites to identify the ritual blueprint for a typical dating event, speed dating, as an example of how these events can be conceptualised as ritual rites of passage. Similar to a service blueprinting which maps hospitality experiences using stages including service encounter, pre-encounter and post-encounter, and action carried out by staff and customers (Bowie et al., 2017), a ritual blueprint has the same role (Figure 2.9).

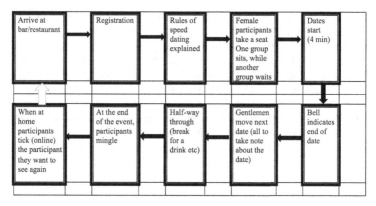

Arrive at bar/restaurant		Registration		Rules of speed dating explained		Female participants take a seat One group sits, while another group waits		Dates start (4 min)	
When at home participants tick (online) the participant they want to see again		At the end of the event, participants mingle		Half-way through (break for a drink etc)		Gentlemen move next date (all to take note about the date)		Bell indicates end of date	

Figure 2.9 Speed dating events ritual blueprinting.

Other rituals exist in dating events in hospitality settings that can also be blueprinted as part of the rite of passage including drunk Jenga; squid game; video game, lock key, naked parties and others (DateinaDash [Online]); SpeedDater [Online]). This ritualistic perspective on bars and restaurants shed light on the dichotomy between the representation that the hospitality industry markets of bars and restaurants as venues associated with primary and secondary cues (Bowie et al., 2017; George, 2021; Hudson & Hudson, 2017; Sloan, Legrand & Chen, 2013; Zeng, De Vries & Go, 2019), and how customers, and dating event businesses are representing and using the space for its social, meta-hospitable role. The intersectionality of dating events helps to reconcile both perceptions and uses of the hospitality space.

2.3.6   *Dating Events and Hospitality Service Quality*

Service quality in hospitality is a multi-dimensional construct, which covers: reliability (what has been promised to be delivered to the customer needs to be delivered); tangibles (customers base their judgement on what they see i.e. physical appearance of the venue, equipment, comfort, etc.); responsiveness (how quickly the organisation addresses requests from their customers); assurance (how trustworthy staff and the organisation are perceived as by customers); and empathy (the level of personalisation of the experience) (Bowie et al., 2017). When these dimension of service quality are not attained, there are service quality gaps due to: knowledge gaps (when customers' expectations are not known); standard gaps (the discrepancy between the service produced and delivered and the expectation of customers); delivery gaps (when the standard of the product or service does not meet the standard expected by customers); the communication gap (when the organisation over-promises on what is going to be delivered and failed to reach the standard); and the perception gap (the discrepancy between what customers expect and what is actually delivered to them) (Bowie et al., 2017).

Dating events have not been investigated by academic research in hospitality and to only a limited extent in events research, nor by the industry itself, as only a limited number of bars and restaurants are working with speed dating event organisers, without a systematic approach or acknowledge strategic partnerships in this area. For example, if we consider the fact that an organisation such as *DateinaDash* (a company founded in 2011 which counts 60,000 active members) who deliver speed dating events 5 days a week and all year round in London, a city with a population of more than 9 million people, only 22 bars and restaurants have partnered with them to date (Table 2.1).

From a hospitality industry perspective, there is a knowledge gap regarding dating events which will inevitably lead to delivery and communication gaps, and yet, there is demand from this type of products and services from the customers. Research in London (see below) shows that the hospitality industry has not yet invested in delivering their own dating events as these are delivered at the moment by dating industry organisations. Investing in dating events as an example of a meta-hospitality practice could be beneficial for hospitality, particularly during crises which affect its performance, because the dating industry is more resilient due to its provision of events with a ritualistic function. Indeed, during the COVID-19 pandemic, the performance of the hospitality industry decreased while the dating industry maintained a steady performance (Statista, 2023 [Online]). The next section of this chapter presents exploratory lexicometric analysis of TripAdvisor reviews related to dating events, to illustrate the conceptual analysis provided this far.

2.3.7   *Customer Perspectives on Dating Events in Hospitality Settings*

This section is based on reviews and replies to these reviews posted on *TripAdvisor* by customers who attended speed dating events organised by *DateinaDash* in London in 2022 (see Figure 2.10). TripAdvisor is one of the most popular social media platforms, with more than 350 million reviews posted per month (Song, Jai & Li, 2018). This platform is usually used to share travel and hospitality experiences (Yu, Li & Jai, 2017), and is regularly used for research which investigates customers' experiences (Moro et al., 2019; Yi, Li & Jai, 2018). *DateinaDash* is the only dating event with a *TripAdvisor* presence, and has received only 40 reviews, highlighting once more the lack of formal organisational integration between dating, hospitality and events, despite the intersectional issues outlined above.

Table 2.1 Examples of bars/restaurants hosting dating events

Venues (restaurants/bars) London areas	Type of events	Other facts about dating events
The Goat		+£10–20
The Piano Works	+Drunk Jenga Dating	+18–60
Ten London	+Single Parties	+London & Online
Forge	+Singles Pub Crawl	+Tuesday to Saturday
The viaduct	+Squid Game Dating	
Luxe	+Gay Speed dating	
Shaka Zulu	+Video Game	
All Bar One	+Naked	
Nordic Bar	+Ball pit	
The Perseverance	+Lock & Key	
Barbican	+Virtual speed dating	
1989 Clubhouse		
LSQ Rooftop		
One Kew Road		
The Roxy		
Ours		
Madison		
The Windmill		
The Sun		
The Goat		
El Vino		
Four Quarters		

Source: The authors (adapted from DateinaDash [Online]) – as of 07.11.22

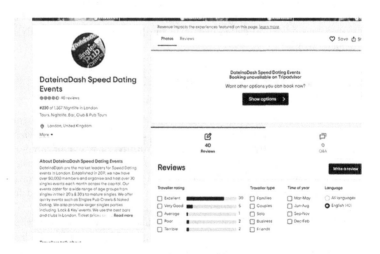

Figure 2.10 Reviews of speed dating experiences on *TripAdvisor.*
Source: TripAdvisor.

Table 2.2 AnaText analysis (comments from consumers)

Ranking	Word	Frequency
1	event	38
2	great	41
3	date	25
4	fun	23
5	venue	20
6	night	33
7	recommend	17
8	organise	16
9	host	14
10	people	30
11	single	15
12	evening	13
13	crawl	9
14	virtual	8
15	attend	11
16	lockdown	4
17	location	9
18	pub	10
19	meet	17
20	shot	11
21	speed	10
22	good	23
23	refund	5
24	first	7
25	friendly	7
26	experience	10
27	alot	3
28	organiser	5
29	free	10
30	atmosphere	5
31	lot	6
32	awesome	3
33	don't	2
34	ppl	1
35	relax	4
36	chatty	2
37	helpful	3
38	everyone	6
39	drink	6
40	queue	3
41	mix	4
42	friend	7
43	whistle	3
44	cancellation	2
45	get	17
46	online	4
47	enjoy	5
48	mingle	2

(*Continued*)

Table 2.2 (Continued)

Ranking	Word	Frequency
49	partial	2
50	value	5
51	scammer	1
52	anyone	5
53	entry	3
54	miscommunication	1
55	ease	3
56	enjoyable	2
57	nice	4
58	icebreaker	1
59	way	10
60	badge	2
61	super	3
62	antic	1
63	etc.	2

Table 2.3 AnaText analysis (comments from organiser)

Ranking	Word	Frequency
1	event	41
2	review	23
3	Thank	18
4	please	18
5	pleased	8
6	thank	14
7	enjoy	16
8	crawl	9
9	feedback	7
10	date	11
11	speed	10
12	pub	9
13	single	11
14	hear	14
15	glad	6
16	lot	7
17	positive	6
18	future	8
19	attend	6
20	recommend	5
21	venue	5
22	experience	7
23	organise	4
24	kind	6
25	great	8
26	regard	4

(*Continued*)

Table 2.3 (Continued)

Ranking	Word	Frequency
27	fun	4
28	com	3
29	appreciate	3
30	provide	5
31	customer	4
32	term	4
33	word	5
34	ratio	2
35	lockdown	1
36	evening	3
37	cancel	2
38	business	5
39	meet	5
40	familiarise	1
41	scorecard	1
42	time	9
43	attendee	1

The reviews were then analysed using *AnaText*, software providing lexico-metric analysis, which combines textual and statistical analysis (Montargot, Kallumuenzer & Kraus, 2022). AnaText enables a lexical analysis of the most recurrent words of a text 'based on similarity, specificity and co-occurrence analyses consists of studying the statistical associations of lemmas or root words, favouring a maieutic of meaning' (Montargot, Kallumuenzer & Kraus, 2022: 3382).

Table 2.2 provides a list of the most recurrent words in the comments from speed daters, while Table 2.3 provides the most recurrent words in the reply from the organiser (*DateinaDash*) to the speed dating events' attendees.

Individuals attending speed dating events, enjoy the experience as 35/40 reviews (87.5%) are grading the events as excellent/very good (see Figure 2.10). Additionally, some of the most cited words in the reviews are related to the venue. Indeed, if we consider the top-tier words in Table 2.3, it reveals that 'Venue' (ranked 5) – and related words such as 'Pub' and 'location' are the most important aspect of the event for customers, because of their ranking and the number of related words in the top-tier of the list.

This was an organised and well-run event which was well attended. The **venue** is a nice **pub** in Richmond. **Great** way to meet people.

These types of events were revealed to be particularly appreciated during lockdown:

Fun way to spend a **lockdown** evening.

Speed dating events also give individuals who are single an opportunity to be part of a group, therefore giving them a sense of belonging:

Enjoyable **singles** evening
Enjoy and meet **single** people!

In terms of rite, the data collected is confirming that this type of event is contributing to move from a particular status not wished (single) to a wished one (in a relationship or married):

I've been to lots of the in-person events and now online events during the lockdown. Haven't found my **husband** yet, but got to speak to lots of people and gave me something to do of an evening regardless.

Keywords from the lexicometric analysis relate to the ritual blueprint, shown in Table 2.3:

Nice venue, well run, good host and friendly and welcoming atmosphere. I had about 10 to 15 **dates**, half time in the **middle** for a **drink** top up. And then **mingle** afterwards, great experience Would I recommend – yes Would I return – yes
The host was fine, but he made little effort with anyone. Blew his **whistle** (Felt like I was back at school again) every **4 mins** and that's about it. In the end, he said we could stay for **drinks** and continue to talk, which is fine, but not in this location.

This second quotation the location of the ritual experience is highlighted as factor that can be changed, indicating the orthodox nature of the dating experience, and the ways in which this can be affected positively or negatively by the hospitality setting, highlighting the intersectionality of events and hospitality taking place through this social practice.

From a business perspective, the level of satisfaction of customers; the significant role that the venue plays in this satisfaction, and the fact that attendees are happy to recommend this type of event, are encouraging.

It was a great experience and lots of fun. I would highly **recommend** this to anyone. Really well organised.
Thanks for the feedback, I am pleased to hear you would **recommend** our business over dating apps.

The importance of hospitality venues for dating events was again shown by the fact that, for one event, it had to be changed. The explanation of the organiser highlights a gap between the hospitality industry and the dating industry which suggests that the optimal hybrid structure for these events suggested by Fragnière and Simon's (2019) hub and satellite approach has not yet been realised in practice.

Thank you for your feedback, unfortunately sometimes **venues do change** due to circumstances beyond our control. I take on board your feedback about the venue and will feed this back to management.

This case indicates a communication gap and a perception gap, as predicted in the discussion of service quality issues and dating events in hospitality settings, above. The intersectional nature of dating events, and the evident reconciliation challenge presented to the hospitality, events and dating industries by this requires further investigation and the following section discusses a research agenda to address this issue.

2.4 Illuminating Dating Events in Hospitality Settings from a Co-Creation of Product and Service Perspective

2.4.1 Overview

Existing research on modern romantic love (Mackinnon, 2022) is essentially covered from a social and technology perspective (Alexopoulos, Timmermans & McNallie, 2020), (Blackwell, Birnholtz & Abbot, 2015), new information perspectives (Gunter, 2008), social and personal relationships perspective (Finkel, Eastwick & Matthews, 2007; Houser, Horan & Furler, 2008) and a discourse perspective (Korobov, 2011).

In the context of a discourse of love (Manghani, 2017), speed dating, from an event management perspective has been totally overlooked. Despite the fact speed dating is a type of recreational event, and probably one of the most popular type of events with people from different age, gender, social background, sexual orientation, etc. (Finkel, Eastwick & Matthews, 2007; Houser, Horan & Furler, 2008, Korobov, 2011; (Dateina-Dash [Online]); SpeedDater [Online]), it is not covered at all in Events Management literature. The same could be said about literature in hospitality management literature. Indeed, if we take the example of the United Kingdom (UK), on the platform Eventbrite, it is some 750 dating events which are advertised every year (Eventbrite [Online]), all hosted in bars and restaurants (DateinaDash [Online]; SpeedDater [Online]). From an Events Management and Hospitality Management perspective, there is a gap in literature when it comes to speed dating events. There is also a gap in literature when it comes to the reconciliation of both the dating and the hospitality industries, as there is no academic literature at all discussing both industries jointly.

This chapter is addressing gaps in literature by investigating speed dating events from a ritual perspective to both conceptualise speed dating as a type of event and investigate the hospitality industry from a new and innovative perspective. In this chapter, ritual which is to be understood as 'any form of repeated action that takes place at a regular and set time' (Andrews & Leopold, 2013: 29), is to be discussed alongside the concept of play. Manghani (2017: 209) pointed out play as being a part of the ritual in modern romantic love interaction. Indeed, he argues that it 'plays its part in amorous exchange and argues how it has the capacity to enable individuals to affirm their own private thoughts, feelings and anxieties'.

Play is also sometimes connected with performance and is happening in a variety of contexts (Powell, Cory & Datillo, 2004). This concept is particularly suited when discussing speed dating events, and more generally speaking romantic relationships, as both involve a certain level of performance in the telling of the type of person we are (Hollenbaugh, 2021; Lewis, 2017; Rui & Stefanone, 2013). This performance is covered in hospitality research through the concept of self-presentation (Catrett & Lynn, 1999). Still in terms of gaps addressed by this chapter, it could also be mentioned the fact that it is investigating two industries as the same time (hospitality and dating), and the intersectional service of both industries.

As this chapter is positing that speed dating events (hosted by bars/restaurants) are adult play comprising rituals, the objective of this research is therefore threefold:

a   To conceptualise speed dating events
b   To provide a perspective of the hospitality industry (bars/restaurants) which is focusing more on the emotional dimension of the industry, namely, social interaction among guests, and other types of interactions happening within the venue during the events
c   To conceptualise the synergy among the dating industry; the hospitality industry; and participants to speed dating events

Existing research in hospitality tends to focus on the operational and commercial aspects of the industry (Lugosi, 2008). The *'marriage à la mode'* dating industry and hospitality industry is offering an opportunity to approach the hospitality industry from a different perspective.

This observatory and participatory chapter is articulated around three research questions:

What contributes to a successful speed dating event?

From a structure point of view, the chapter starts with an attempt to conceptualise both speed dating events, and the relationship dating industry and hospitality industry. This is done using the concept of play as a thread. Once these relationships conceptualised, they will be explored. Therefore, the second part of this section of the chapter discusses the methodology (observation and participation) used to test the theory developed (conceptualisation of speed dating events, and the relationship dating industry and hospitality industry). Finally, the discussion and concluding remarks section identifies is articulated around four sections: (1) the identification and discussion of factors contributing to the speed dating experience (2) a recap of how the research questions and objectives of the chapter have been addressed (3) the academic and practical contributions of the chapter are clearly highlighted (4) and finally, a research agenda is offered.

2.4.2 *Play*

Play is most of the time associated with fun and children (Poris, 2006). Indeed, as a form of communication, play is an important part in the life of children as they learn as they play (Resnick, 2004). This is referred to as edutainment (education and entertainment) or playful learning (Resnick, 2004). *KidZania* is an example of organisation offering serious leisure, or playful learning to children (Tagg & Wang, 2016; Di Pietro et al., 2018). Play also tells many things about children: Who they are as a person; their level of imagination; their ability to understand and follow rules; their ability to engage and interact with others; to develop and nurture some feeling; etc. (Lewis, 2017; Powell, Cory & Datillo, 2004). Despite the important role of play in the life of children (Lewis, 2017; Poris, 2006), it is not unanimously considered as important. For some it is just a whimsical correlated with health and safety issues, and noisy behaviour (Lewis, 2017).

From a theoretical point of view, play as a phenomenon (Holst, 2017) has been conceptualised through the different dimensions of fun (Poris, 2006): sport orientated; friend orientated; empowering; creative; silly; family orientated; relaxing and rebellious. Based on this classification, and based on the key characteristics and benefits of play (mentioned in the preceded paragraph), such as communication tool, playful learning, development of imagination, interaction, etc. (Holst, 2017; Kerr & Moore, 2015; Resnick, 2004), play can't just be considered as an activity for children, as some of its key features and benefits are also acknowledged in adult centric environments (Deterding, 2018; Heuser, 2004; Scott & Godbey, 1992). This chapter is exclusively focusing on adult play.

Heuser (2004) explains that play in an adult centric environment contributes to the building of a community among the individuals involved (regardless their gender, age, social and professional situation, and physical condition). This view of play as contributing to the development of social capital, engagement, connectedness, etc., among individuals is also shared by Harris and Daley (2008), and by Baxter (2016), who are arguing that play can bridge the gap between individuals and/or groups.

Table 2.4 Examples of keywords associated with play

A	B	C	D
What it is about	*What is required*	*Outcome/results (positive)*	*Outcomes/results (limitation)*
Communication tool	Interaction	Reveals personality	Reveals personality
Learning tool	Rules	Feeling	Feeling
Fun	Imagination	Community	Health and safety
Socialisation	Fun environment	Social capital	behaviour
Resistance/ activism	Fantasy	Inclusion	
Social or serious	Abandon of rational behaviour	Performance	
Metrics		Mood	
Adaptation		Energy	
Social and cultural construct		Positive emotion	
Ritual		Satisfaction	

Adult play can happen in a variety of contexts, such as:

The working environment. In the working environment, Celestine and Yeo (2020) have explained that play has an array of benefits such as improvement of performance, better mood and boost of energy. Other benefits of adult play include learning and socialisation (Shen, Chick & Pitas, 2017).

Play is also associated with romantic relationships, in the sense that in a relationship, it contributes to the positive emotion between the partners, therefore contributing to relationship satisfaction (Aune & Wong, 2002). For this level of emotion and satisfaction to happen, Turley, Monro and King (2017) are explaining that a good imagination, fun environment and participants with some fantasies are required.

Adult play could also be perceived as a form of resistance to a situation, or a context (Myers, 2016). In other words, a form of passive activism, that Tranter (2010) defines as a form of activism which happens behind the scenes, and does not require a form of protests, etc.

To better understand adult play, and more importantly, to conceptualise it, academics have developed models, among these are:

Celestine and Yeo (2020) model. They have developed a typology with four categories of play: work-embedded play; self-/peer-initiated work-embedded play; manager-initiated diversionary play and self-/peer-initiated diversionary play.

Scott and Godbey (1992) are offering a more simplistic segmentation of play. Indeed, for them, play is either social or serious. The main difference being how the participants are selected; the characteristics of the participants; the main purpose of the activity; the type of game which is played; etc.

Having a good understanding of play is important, as the level of playfulness of an individual (or organisation) is also considered as a metrics to evaluate the ability to adapt to a context, situation, etc. (Shen, Chick & Pitas, 2017). That said, play is not a panacea. Barnett (2017) highlighted the cultural and social dimension of play. According to the country or culture, play does not have the same value and importance. In some culture, it is a family legacy, with rituals as a transmission process (Barnett, 2017). The idea of play being a social construct is also shared by Voogt (2017). It is also worth mentioning that like children play (Lewis, 2017), adult play also has some negative aspects such as cost, injury, predation, waste of time (Shen, Chick & Pitas, 2017).

The preceded review of literature on play, supported by research carried out by Baxter (2016) and Myers (2016) has revealed that children play, and adult play have many similarities. The review has also pointed out keywords associated with play, which has facilitated the development of the typology presented in Table 2.4.

Based on Table 2.4, this chapter is adopting the following definition of play by Van Vleet and Feeney (2015: 632), who define play as

An **activity** that is carried out for the purpose of **amusement and fun**, that is approached with **enthusiastic** and in-the-moment **attitude**, that is highly **interactive**.

2.4.3   *Play from an Events Management Literature Perspective*

The perceived experience model developed by Edger and Oddy (2018), which has four interlocking spheres: Event (entertainment, performance, occasion, ancillary products/services), service (speed, knowledge, warmth, sociability, politeness, rectification), price (cost), venue (atmosphere, design, facilities, comfort, layout, setting); and at the intersection of the four spheres can be found 'perceived experience' (customer satisfaction, positive advocacy). As play falls under 'event', and as such it is directly connected with service, price and venue, and impacts on the experience of customers.

The phenomenon of play and events management studies are closely related. They are reconciliated through their socio-cultural dimension (Andrews & Leopold, 2013; Voogt, 2017). Other aspects reconciling both include rituals, educational dimension, entertainment, and fostering community (Andrews & Leopold, 2013; Barnett, 2017; Resnick, 2004; Turley, Monro & King, 2017). In that sense, play has many similarities with Carnival which is a cultural and community events (Quinn, 2013) defined as:

An annual festival involving **processions, music, dancing**, and the use of **masquerade, inversion**.

(Quinn, 2013: 5)

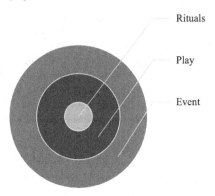

Figure 2.11 Event, play and rituals as components of the engagement model.

Indeed, both play and Carnival are expressing through rituals a certain form of hedonism, a certain abandon of rational behaviour, and excess (Quinn, 2013). Both play and Carnival offer the opportunity to meet new people, and be involved in new activities (Barnett, 2017; Quinn, 2013; Resnick, 2004; Turley, Monro & King, 2017).

From a ritual perspective, literature in events management studies (Andrews & Leopold, 2013) reveals that play could be considered as a rite of passage, as it represents sometimes the transition between children and adulthood; or the transition from a physical ability to inability, etc. (Heuser, 2004); rite of reversal, as for some adults, play is a way to return to their childhood, even if it is for a short moment (Baxter, 2016); rite of conspicuous display, as some adult play such as consensual bondage are quite based on senses, are non-conventional, and are based on physical and psychological sensations (Turley, Monro & King, 2017); Rite of exchange due to the social aspect of play (Voogt, 2017), and rite of competition, as some play are based on competition (Poris, 2006).

Reading at the preceding information regarding the features of both play and events, each has a strong potential in term of engagement. Indeed, they could each be considered as drivers of engagement. Combined (play and events), their potential in terms of engagement is doubled (Figure 2.11). Indeed, for Edger and Oddy (2018), engagement in events management is related to: positive relationship between partners involved; a high level of commitment; and an increase of performance.

2.4.4   *Play from a Hospitality Management Literature Perspective*

The hospitality industry is essentially presented as an industry based on experience and well-being, which can happen either through accommodation;

through the food and beverage provided; or through entertainment (Lugosi, 2008). Entertainment is part of the services offered by the hospitality industry to customers (George, 2021; Sloan, Legrand & Chen, 2013). Entertainment is also important to the industry as it plays a role in the attainment of what is referred as the meta-hospitality or ultimate flow experience (Kim, Whaley & Choi, 2022; Lugosi, 2008). This practically translates into customers enjoying themselves, interacting with each other, coming back and recommending the venue to others (Kim, Whaley & Choi, 2022; Lugosi, 2008).

Based on the preceded sections, this chapter is positing two things. First, entertainment (intersection) and related outcomes are reconciling the hospitality industry, events management and play. Second, that for the engagement potential of play and events to be maximised, an appropriate physical environment is needed.

Research from Bowie et al. (2017) has highlighted the fact that in the hospitality industry the physical environment plays a significant role in attracting and retaining customers. Equally important, Bowie et al. (2017) have pointed out that the physical environment plays a role on the behaviour of customers. Indeed, if the latter feel comfortable in their environment, they will develop and display an approach behaviour, which translates into them spending more money, coming back to the venue and recommend it to others. It also translates into two types of emotional responses, namely arousal (being alert, excited, energised) and pleasure (enjoyment, happiness/euphoria). If they do not feel comfortable, they develop an avoidance behaviour, which translates into not being tempted to enter the venue. Bowie et al. (2017) are therefore emphasising the importance of the use of space, seating arrangement, décor, lighting and background music as stimuli (visual, aural, tactile, olfactory) as central in the success of a venue (fostering social interaction, enjoyment, repeat customers, etc.)

2.4.5   Play, Hospitality Industry and Speed Dating Events

The dating industry which offers two main types of products and services, namely dating apps (Alexopoulos, Timmermans & McNallie, 2020), and speed dating events (Turowetz & Hollander, 2012) is both physical and digital (phygital) industry. As a new emerging experiential model (Johnson & Barlow, 2021), which appeared for the first time in 2013 (Mele & Russo-Spena, 2021), phygitalisation has a strong potential in terms of engaging and enhancing the experience of customers (Baratta et al., 2022; Mele & Russo-Spena, 2021), fostering a context for the development of new opportunities for businesses (Mele & Russo-Spena, 2021), and subsequently improving their competitiveness (Ballina, Valdes & Del Valle, 2019). In the UK alone, the dating industry is worth £315 million (Ibisworld [Online]).

Speed-dating event is an interplay experiential product and service between the dating industry and the hospitality industry. Indeed, as an industry, the dating industry develops products and services which are offering users the possibility to meet potential new partners, most of the time virtually (Alexopoulos, Timmermans & McNallie, 2020), and then physically in bars and restaurants (BBC[Online]), which are falling under the hospitality industry (Lugosi, 2008). As a type of event (Finkel & Eastwick, 2008; Korobov, 2011) speed dating falls under many categories of the typology of planned events developed by Getz and Page (2020). Indeed, speed dating could fall under both, private functions (which includes among others 'parties'); and recreation (which also includes 'fun events'). The worldwide success of this type of event with individuals of all age, background, gender, religion, etc. (Finkel & Eastwick, 2008; Korobov, 2011; Turowetz & Hollander, 2012) could be explained by the fact that individuals are very busy with their daily life and subsequently have less time to make romantic encounters (Houser, Horan & Furler, 2008).

As a provider of entertainment, accommodation, food and beverage (Hudson & Hudson, 2017; Lugosi, 2008), the hospitality sector is accommodating speed dating events organised by Speed dating companies (Dateina-Dash [Online]); SpeedDater [Online]). This view of speed-dating being an interplay between both industries is also shared by the founder of the dating app *Thursday* who argued that dating apps should just be about putting two people in touch, and the real encounters should happen in bars and restaurants (BBC[Online]). The hospitality industry is offering to users of the dating industry a physical context suited for entertainment, which enables the attainment of some emotions.

Speed dating could also be considered as a social and serious play with some rules, as described below by Finkel and Eastwick (2008: 193):

'Individuals interested in **meeting** potential romantic partners go on approximately 10 to 25 very brief (e.g.,4-minute) "dates" with a series of **desired-sex partners**. After the event, participants **report** whether they would ("yes") or would not ("no") be interested in corresponding with each speed-dating partner again in the future. If two participants reply "yes" to each other, they are a **match**, and the host of the speed-dating event provides them with the opportunity to **contact each other**, perhaps to arrange a more **traditional date**.'

Socialisation and the development of interconnection among participants is the main purpose of speed dating events. This type of events could be considered as rite of passage (from single to having a partner); rite of conspicuous display (display of emotions); rite of exchange (exchange of contact details); rite of competition (the purpose is to 'win' at least one match to go on a date). The right choice of venue to hold speed dating events should contribute to enhance the quality of experience due to the capacity of a venue arousing and pleasuring potential (Bowie et al., 2017).

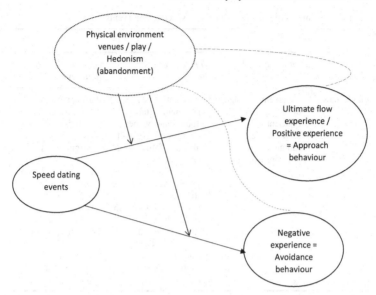

Figure 2.12 Speed dating and potential impacts on the hospitality industry.

Based on preceded information provided in this chapter, it could be argued that the physical environment of bars/restaurants (use of space, seating arrangement, décor, lighting and background music) plays a significant role in the speed dating experience (which might also include participants matching with a partner). In that case the customer would display an approach behaviour. Similarly, it could be argued that the physical environment of the venue could play the total opposite role, i.e. a negative experience (which might also include participants not matching with a partner), which might translate into an avoidance behaviour. The venue could therefore be considered as a moderating factor impacting on the potential of a play (Figure 2.12). By hosting speed dating events (serious and social adult play), bars and restaurants (venue) are also potentially putting their image, reputation, performance at a stake.

2.4.6   *Methods and Results*

To investigate speed dating events, Table 2.5 provides a list of key points to observe.

To assess speed dating events using the above-listed parameters (Table 2.2), the author of this chapter attended a speed dating event (Figure 2.4). Therefore, from a methodological point of view, this exploratory chapter has adopted both an observation and participation role. Lugosi (2008) adopted a similar approach

Table 2.5 Examples of parameters to assess speed dating events

A	B	C	
What it is about	*What is required*	*Outcome/results (positive)*	*Outcomes/results (limitation)*
Play/rituals	Physical environment or venue (fun, Pleasant, comfortable, romantic environment, etc.)	Participants reveal their personality (talk about fantasy, they are relaxed, gradually abandon formal tone behaviour, etc.)	Participants are not relaxed, they remain on their guard, the tone is formal, etc.)
		All participants are involved and bonding	Some participants are on the fence
		Participants are in a good mood, seems to be satisfied	Health and safety issues
		Overall, there is a sense of positive energy	The atmosphere is unfriendly
		Participants are exchanging details, etc.	No real interaction / bonding among participants

when investigating the interaction among customers and staff of a bar in Budapest (Hungary). This observation and participation approach provide useful insights that one would not get if done differently (Lugosi, 2006, 2008).

From observation and participation, a thick description of the event is provided (Section 4). The description is based on the parameters listed in Table 2.2. As a methodological approach, thick description is defined as (Leeds-Hurwitz, 2015: 860–868):

A **detailed description** of **actual behaviour,** typically resulting from ethnography, sufficient to permit the reader to **see below surface appearances** by offering an **understanding of underlying patterns and context** that give the information meaning.

The keywords from the definition of thick description are echoing what was discussed for play, events and hospitality. For Redding (2015), thick description enables to unravel some situations, and therefore provides intelligibly covered information. Thick description was used by Lugosi (2008) in a hospitality context (described earlier).

2.4.6.1   *Thick Description: Speed Dating Event, Las Iguanas, Basingstoke (UK), 22 November 2022 (19:30–22:30)*

The venue (restaurant) for the event was easy to find as within a shopping centre. However, when I arrived, I was not sure it was the right place because people (customers) were having their meal in the restaurant. Moreover, there was no indication (sign or staff) about the event. I waited by the bar, then a lady (the organiser) came by, and indicated where the event would be taking place (floor/mezzanine above). Because the room was not ready yet, she suggested that I had drink while waiting. I ordered mineral water (I really did not like the taste of it). Once done, a few minutes later, I made my way upstairs. I found it really embarrassing having to cross the restaurant to go to the upper floor. I had the feeling that the customers (having their meal) were staring at me.

Once upstairs, by the bar (there are two bars in the venue), the event organiser came by. She checked me in, gave me a badge (a sticker with my name handwritten on it), a (branded) pen and a (branded) card to record the name of the ladies, the table number, etc. Basically, the rule of speed dating was explained clearly with sufficient details.

As I was one of the first one to check-in, the organiser suggested that I buy another drink or something to eat (downstairs) while waiting for the start of the event. I took this opportunity to have a look around the upper floor. Overall, it was a very small room in a 'L' shape. In terms of decoration, it was a small room with some tables (with very minimal and basic Christmas decoration). One of the sides of the room opens on the downstair restaurant. When you walk into the room, there is bar (rather shabby) on the left-hand side, some toilets next to it. There were 14 tables round the room. On each table there was a candle. One of the tables was wobbling. That was rather annoying.

While having my drink and waiting for the event to start, I had a very nice chat with the event organiser. She was very friendly and nice. She told me about all the events she organises. She told me about the success stories of her events, she even invited me to attend her next event (in Winchester).

When the participants arrived, they registered and went straight to a table or stood around the bar. There was not much conversation going among participants. Quite a few participants came with their friends. I also came with a (female) friend. Altogether we were 28 participants (14 male/14 female) in our 30s and 40s. When it was the time, and everyone had arrived, the organiser rang a bell and asked for our attention. She explained the rule of the speed dating event (women stay at the table, men move around, each speed dating is 4 minutes, then a break halfway through, etc.).

The organiser rang the bell and the event started. Very quickly the small room got very noisy. It was sometimes very difficult to hear the other person. So, we had to shout or get closer. Some of the participants (women) were taking it seriously as taking notes during the date. Other like me, took it easy and focused primarily on the conversation. The conversations were very basic (all focused on work, hobby, address, etc.). With some participants there were a good vibe as sharing jokes and having a laugh). During the break, some people mingled, but most of the ladies remained seated. The people who came with their friends got together. Having said that, the size of the room did not really

eventbrite

Speed Dating in Basingstoke for 30s & 40s
Gents ticket £24.30

Las Iguanas - Basingstoke (Upstairs Bar), Festival Place, Festival Way, Basingstoke RG21
7BB, United Kingdom

Tuesday, 22 November 2022 from 19:30 to 22:30 (GMT)

Eventbrite Completed

Order information

Order #5088106689. Ordered by Hugues SERAPHIN on 6 November 2022 17:30

50881066898237737719001

Figure 2.13 Attendance to a speed dating event.
Source: Eventbrite/the author.

help in terms of gathering. One of the participants (women) even left before the end of the event (during the 20 minutes break, halfway through the event).

At the end of the event, the organiser explained how to record our choices on the website, etc. The participants left almost immediately. No one seemed to be overly excited. The event organiser left rather quickly as well (she cleaned the room a bit, gathered her belongings, etc.). Only two people (male and female – the friend I came with) stayed behind (20 minutes roughly). On the speed dating website, and on the ticket (Figure 2.3), it says that the event would last 3 hours (1930–2230). The event finished at 2130 (1 hour earlier).

Out of all the participants (female) only one stood out for me. On top of her very pleasant physical appearance, she was natural. She came with her niece. She even joked about it (family support, etc.). During the 4 minutes we kept cracking jokes about everything. All the other participants (female), even if they were nice, polite, etc., they all went by the book, and stick to the scenario (question/answer).

As for the venue, the downstairs restaurant was nice. But the upper floor (mezzanine) where the event happened was disappointed, because of its size, the level of comfort, the design, appearance, etc. Overall, it was an average experience. Having said that, I would not mind attending another speed dating event (Figure 2.13).

2.4.7   *Discussion and Concluding Remarks*

This section is discussing the key factors framing speed dating as a type of event organised by the dating industry but held in a hospitality context. The results of the observation and participation approach are in line with the theoretical findings summarised in Table 2.2. Indeed, both the conceptual and empirical findings are suggesting there are free core factors framing speed dating events: (1) Ecology or physical environment; (2) Roles or casting – many players and one play master; (3) The capability of the participants to abandon themselves to hedonism.

This chapter is also acknowledging the work from Lugosi (2008) who identified three core factors (ecology, roles, and capability) contributing to a positive environment in a hospitality context. The main difference between this chapter and the chapter carried out by Lugosi (2008) is the involvement of customers. Indeed, in the case of speed dating events, customers are also participants (active customers), while in the case of Lugosi (2008) customers were passive, as they were just attending a performance (piano and singing) delivered by the third party. In both cases, it appears that the factors contributing to the overall experience are the same.

The core factors contributing to the speed dating experience:

2.4.7.1   The Ecology (or Physical Environment/Servicescape)

The perception of the servicescape plays a role in the impression formed by customers, which then translates into emotions (Lin, 2004), such as the pleasure level (Lin & Mattila, 2010) or the opposite. The perception of servicescape is a good indicator of what the customer attitude, satisfaction, consumption, and advocacy is going to be (Hanks & Line, 2018). Among the cues of servicescape in hospitality that matter the most for customers are aesthetics, the atmospheric, space/function, seating comfort, cleanliness, etc. (Lee, Wang & Cai, 2018). Equally important, Reimer and Kuehn (2004) are arguing the impact of servicescape on customer satisfaction is more important in hedonistic service (compared with utilitarian service). Having said that, Lugosi (2008) also added the fact that the impact of servicescape is moderated by the participation of customers, and more generally speaking, by the dynamic among all stakeholders involved in the event (Kralj & Solnet, 2010).

This literature is in line with Bowie et al. (2017) research on customer behaviour in the hospitality sector discussed in Section 2.3 of this chapter. This literature on servicescape is also in line with the thick description of the speed dating event (Section 4), in the sense that the size of the venue and its design did not really contribute (to the extent it could have), to the fostering of interaction among participants. As speed dating is a hedonistic service (due to its connection with play, fun, events and pleasure), servicescape is even more important. Equally important, at the speed dating event, some participants came with their 'own community' (of family and friends), which did not help with a creation of a dynamic among participants.

2.4.7.2   Roles or Casting (Players and Play Master)

In speed dating events, the organiser (play master) is first and foremost a facilitator who ensures rules are understood and followed by everyone. The main actors are the speed daters. They play alongside the physical environment a major role in the overall experience. The play dimension is very much present in speed dating events. Indeed, (1) at the beginning of the event the rules are explained; (2) players/daters are provided with a score card and at the end of the event, when participants have entered their choices, the number of matches are communicated to participants; (3) the dates are the actual play time; (4) the rites involved in the event (as discussed in Section 2.4) are also part of what contributes to make speed dating a type of (serious/social) play.

*2.4.7.3   The Capability of the Participants to Abandon
          Themselves to Hedonism*

If we consider the example of Carnival (Quinn, 2013), and meta hospitality (Lugosi, 2008), full enjoyment happens when individuals fully abandon themselves to hedonism (Lugosi, 2008; Quinn, 2013). This view is further supported by Demeter, MacInnes and Dolnicar (2022), who are arguing that happiness is often defined using the concepts of eudemonia, which is the ability of an individual to get the best out of the self, and hedonia, which is based on the ability to reach pleasure, enjoyment, and comfort. Both eudemonia and hedonia are influencing behaviour. Both also varies according to the context (Demeter, MacInnes & Dolnicar, 2022). On that basis, servicescape could be said to impact on eudemonia and hedonia. The thick description in Section 4 shows that the venue for the speed dating event was a barrier to the achievement of full eudemonia and hedonia (flow experience/meta hospitality).

As a type of event, speed dating could be defined as both serious and social play, articulated around a certain number of rites (passage, conspicuous display, exchange and competition). The success of the event is based on the physical environment, the roles performed by the different actors, and finally, the capabilities of the participants to abandon themselves to hedonism. Speed dating is therefore a co-created event among three main stakeholders, namely the dating industry (planning and delivering the event), the hospitality industry (hosting the event and contributing to the experience) and finally the participants (co-creators of the experience). The venue (physical environment), type of play (and rites), and the level of abandonment of participants are considered as moderating factors of the type of experience customers are getting, and therefore influencing their behaviour (approach or avoidance behaviour). Figure 2.14 is a model of conceptualisation of speed dating events, showing the synergy among the key stakeholders.

The contributions of this chapter are varied. From a theoretical point of view, this chapter has revealed that in a hospitality context, whether customers are co-creators or co-contributors of the experience at the event, physical

Dating industry

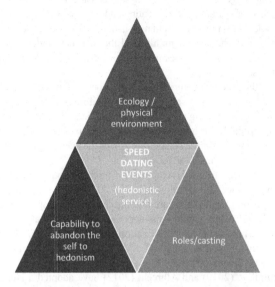

Hospitality industry   Participants

Figure 2.14 Model of conceptualisation of speed dating events, and synergy dating industry, hospitality industry and participants.

environment, roles, and capability are key elements of the success of the event. The chapter has also revealed that these key elements are also moderating factors of the type of experience customers are getting. This chapter could therefore be said to be complementary to Lugosi (2008) as discussing the topic of experience in hospitality from a co-creation and intersection service perspective.

From a theoretical point view, this chapter could also be said to have contributed to the reconciliation of the hospitality and dating industry, through speed dating events (intersection). No other studies had discussed speed dating from a hospitality perspective. The chapter is therefore filling a gap in literature.

Still from a theoretical point of view, this chapter is one of the very few, or maybe the only one focusing on an intersection service. Research tends to focus on services belonging to a specific industry. Speed dating is breaking with existing research in hospitality. This approach is important to further knowledge in an area. Indeed, Brooker and Joppe (2013), are arguing that to unlock situations, radical innovation (as opposed to incremental innovation) is necessary but lacking in some areas such as tourism.

This chapter is contributing to academic literature in events management. Despite the importance of speed dating as a type of event, it is not investigated at all from that perspective. Existing typology of events such as the one developed by Getz and Page (2020) is not taking into consideration events such as speed dating. This chapter has put speed dating under private functions and recreation, out of choice. This typology could now include 'serious and social play'.

Finally, this chapter has highlighted the fact that modern romantic love, does not need to involve technology and can be based on direct human interactions.

As for the practical contribution, it lays on the fact that it is indicating to speed dating event organisers, and to bars and restaurants managers what to focus on when organising speed dating events. Successful speed dating events could be profitable for both as the participants to speed dating events might turn into customers for the restaurants. As for the event organisers, they would benefit from it in terms of advocacy.

When it comes to the development of research agenda, academics do not agree on the procedure to follow:

Dubois and Ceron (2006) are arguing that the development of a research agenda should adopt a four steps approach: (1) identification of the gap in literature; (2) the development of actions to fill the gap; (3) identification of the most suitable research method to do so; (4) identification of the field of chapter to tie the research with.

Maximilian (2019) and Albrecht (2012) have adopted a Nominal Group Technique (NGT), which includes six steps, namely: (1) the generation of ideas, (2) recording the ideas generated, (3) classification of the ideas into themes, (4) identifying through a collegiate vote, which ideas are the most important (5) debate around the selected themes, (6) ranked the selected themes according to their importance and priority.

This chapter is suggesting future research to adopt an approach combining the above-described approaches:

Step 1: Identification of key themes
Step 2: Process of selection and ranking of key themes
Step 3: Critical analysis (using literature) of selected key themes
Step 4: Implications (opportunities, challenges, and solutions) for each key theme

As for future research, they could be looking at a lexicometric analysis of feedback posted by speed daters after attending an event to identify what matters the most for them when attending such an event. Is their focus on the attendees, and interactions? On the venue? On the organisation of the event? What are the cues for the choice of speed dating events to attend?, etc. The lexicometric analysis could be done using a software like ALCESTRE (Montargot, Kallumuenzer & Kraus, 2022). This analysis could be followed by a Factorial Correspondence Analysis (FCA) to identify clusters. This research is important because customers based their decision on cues such as design, atmospheric, space/function, seating comfort, cleanliness, etc. (Lee, Wang & Cai, 2018). This information could be valuable for speed dating event organisers. Having said that, data (reviews of speed daters) are not available online. Only two sets of data seem to be available online to best of the knowledge of the author. There are 40 reviews on *TripAdvisor* (TripAdvisor [Online]) and 355 reviews on *Truspilot.com* (Trustpilot [Online]).

Futures research could also look at if there is a correlation between the three core elements of the success of a speed dating events and the number of matches one get. This question is motivating by Figure 2.5 (performance of the author at the event). It is also worth mentioning that academic research in tourism discussing romance is scarce (Li, He & Qiao, 2021). This might also be the case in hospitality academic research, as hospitality, tourism and event management studies are closely related (Evans, 2020; George, 2021; Okumus et al., 2020).

Another topic of research could be about intersection services. How is the ownership of the industry determined? In the case of speed dating events, the dating industry has taking ownership as speed dating events are planned, promoted, and delivered by speed dating event organisers. The hospitality sector is just a host (bars/restaurants do not even promote on their social media platforms the fact they are hosting this type of event).

References

ABIA. Retrieved from https://abia.org.uk/

Adamczyk, K. (2017). Voluntary and involuntary singlehood and young adults' mental health: An investigation of mediating role of romantic loneliness. *Current Psychology, 36*, 888–904. https://doi.org/10.1007/s12144-016-9478-3

Adamczyk, K. (2018). Direct and indirect effects of relationship status through unmet need to belong and fear of being single on young adults' romantic loneliness. *Personality and Individual Differences, 124*, 124–129. https://doi.org/10.1016/j.paid.2017.12.011

Aguinis, H., Villamor, I., Lazzarini, S. G., Vassolo, R. S., Amoros, J. E., & Allen, D. G. (2020). Conducting management research in Latin America: Why and what's in it for you? *Journal of Management, 46*(5), 615–636.

Albrecht, J. N. (2012). Networking for sustainable tourism – towards a research agenda. *Journal of Sustainable Tourism, 21*(5), 639–657.

Alexopoulos, C., Timmermans, E., & McNallie, J. (2020). Swiping more, committing less: Unravelling the links among dating app use, dating app success, and intention to commit infidelity. *Computers in Human Behaviour, 102*, 172–180.

Altinay, L., Alrawadieh, Z., Tulucu, F., & Arici, H. A. (2023). The effect of hospitableness on positive emotions, experience, and well-being of hospital patients. *International Journal of Hospitality Management, 110*. https://doi.org/10.1016/j.ijhm.2023.103431

Andrews, H., & Leopold, T. (2013). *Events and the social sciences.* London: Routledge.

Aune, K. S., & Wong, N. C. H. (2002). Antecedents and consequences of adult play in romantic relationships. *Personal Relationships, 9*, 279–286.

Ballina, F. J., Valdes, L., & Del Valle, E. (2019). The Phygital experience in the smart tourism destination. *International Journal of Tourism Cities, 5*(4), 656–671.

Bandyopadhyay, R. (2013). A paradigm shift in sex tourism research. *Tourism Management Perspectives, 6*, 1–2.

Baratta, R., Bonfanti, A., Cucci, M. G., & Simeoni, F. (2022). Enhancing cultural tourism through the development of memorable experiences: The "Food Democracy Museum" as a phygital project. *Sinergie, 40*(1), 153–176.

Barnett, L. A. (2017). The inculcation of adult playfulness: From west to east. *International Journal of Play, 6*(3), 255–271.

Bauer, I. L. (2014). Romance tourism or female sex tourism?. *Travel Medicine and Infectious Disease, 12*(1), 20–28.

Baxter, J. E. (2016). Adult nostalgia and children's toys past and present. *International Journal of Play, 5*(3), 230–243.

BBC. The Thursday dating app that only works one day a week. Retrieved from https://www.bbc.co.uk/news/uk-england-gloucestershire-61254921, accessed on 30.06.22

Berdychevsky, L., Gibson, H. J., & Bell, H. L. (2016). "Girlfriend getaway" as a contested term: Discourse analysis. *Tourism Management, 55*, 106–122.

Bernard, S., Rahman, I., & McGehee, N. G. (2022). Breaking barriers for Bangladeshi female solo travelers. *Tourism Management Perspectives, 41*, 100932.

Bianchi, C. (2016). Solo holiday travellers: Motivators and drivers of satisfaction and dissatisfaction. *International Journal of Tourism Research, 18*(2), 197–208.

Bianchi, C. (2022). Antecedents of tourists' solo travel intentions. *Tourism Review, 77*(3), 780–795.

Blackwell, C., Birnholtz, J., & Abbot, C. (2015). Seeing and being seen: Co-situation and impression formation using Grindr, a location-aware gay dating app. *New media & Society, 17*(7), 1117–1136.

Borman, G. (1998). *Orwell's 1984*. Lincoln: Cliffs Notes.

Bowie, D., Buttle, F., Brookes, M., & Mariussen, A. (2017). *Hospitality marketing*. Abingdon: Routledge.

Brooker, E., & Joppe, M. (2013). Trends in camping and outdoor hospitality—An international review. *Journal of Outdoor Recreation and Tourism, 3*(1), 1–6.

Brooker, E., Joppe, M., Davidson, M. C., & Marles, K. (2012). Innovation within the Australian outdoor hospitality parks industry. *International Journal of Contemporary Hospitality Management, 24*(5), 682–700.

Brown, L., & Osman, H. (2017). The female tourist experience in Egypt as an Islamic destination. *Annals of Tourism Research, 63*, 12–22. https://doi.org/10.1016/j.annals.2016.12.005

Brozović, D., & Tregua, M. (2022). The evolution of service systems to service ecosystems: A literature review. *International Journal of Management Reviews, 24*(4), 459–479.

Brugulat, M., & Coromina, L. (2021). Constraints of solo female backpackers in Southeast Asia. *Asia Pacific Journal of Tourism Research, 26*(6), 640–653. https://doi.org/10.1080/10941665.2021.1886134

Bunghez, C. L. (2021). The emerging trend of niche tourism: Impact analysis. *Journal of Marketing Research and Case Studies, 2021*, 134710–134730.

Businessof Apps (2023). Dating App Revenue and Usage Statistics. Retrieved from https://www.businessofapps.com/data/dating-app-market/, accessed on 20.02.23

Carr, N. (2016). Sex in tourism: Reflections and potential future research directions. *Tourism Recreation Research, 41*(2), 188–198. https://doi.org/10.1080/02508281.2 016.1168566

Catrett, J., & Lynn, M. (1999). Managing status in the hotel industry: How four seasons came to the fore. *Cornell Hospitality Quarterly*. https://doi.org/10.1177/001088049904000120

Celestine, N. A., & Yeo, G. (2020). Having some fun with it: A theoretical review and typology of activity-based play-at-work. *Journal of Organisational Behaviour, 42,* 252–268.

Chhetri, A., Chhetri, P., Arrowsmith, C., & Corcoran, J. (2017). Modelling tourism and hospitality employment clusters: A spatial econometric approach. *Tourism Geographies, 19*(3), 398–424.

Chiang, C. Y., & Jogaratnam, G. (2006). Why do women travel solo for purposes of leisure?. *Journal of Vacation Marketing, 12*(1), 59–70.

DatelnaDash. Retrieved from https://www.bighospitality.co.uk/Article/2012/01/26/ Dating-contributes-over-1bn-to-hospitality-industry, accessed on 30.06.22

Demeter, C., MacInnes, S., & Dolnicar, S. (2022). Defining and operationalizing eight forms of eudaimonia and hedonia and assessing tourism-specific context-dependency. *Journal of Travel Research*. https://doi.org/10.1177/00472875221133042

Deterding, S. (2018). Alibis for adult play: A Goffmanian account of escaping embarrassment in adult play. *Games and Culture, 13*(3), 260–279.

d'Hauteserre, A. M. (2004). Postcolonialism, colonialism, and tourism. In Lew, A., Hall, M., & Williams, A. (Eds.), *A companion to tourism* (pp. 235–245). New York: Blackwell Publishing.

Dileep, M. R., & Nair, B. B. (2021). COVID-19 and the future of tourism: back to normal or reformation? *International Journal of Hospitality & Tourism Systems, 14*(1), 1–15.

Di Pietro, L., Edvarsson, B., Reynoso, J., Renzi, M. F., Toni, M., & Mugion, R. G. (2018). A scaling up framework for innovative service ecosystems: Lessons from Eataly and KidZania. *Journal of Service Management, 29*(1), 146–175.

Dubois, G., & Ceron, J. P. (2006). Tourism and climate change: Proposals for a research agenda. *Journal of Sustainable Tourism, 14*(4), 399–415.

Duffy, R., & Smith, M. (2004). *The ethics of tourism development*. Abingdon: Routledge.

Edger, C., & Oddy, R. E. (2018). *Events Management. 87 key models for event, venue and experience (EVE) managers*. Faringdon: Libri Publishing.

Evans, N. (2020). *Strategic management for tourism, hospitality and events*. London: Routledge.

Eventbrite. Retrieved from https://www.eventbrite.co.uk/blog/press/press-releases/new-data-shows-real-life-dating-events-back-en-vogue/

FasterCapital. (2023). *Solo travel bliss: Embracing independence away from home - FasterCapital*. [online] Retrieved from https://fastercapital.com/content/Solo-Travel-Bliss--Embracing-Independence-Away-from-Home.html, accessed on 21.03.24.

Fessman, N., & Lester, D. (2000). Loneliness and depression among elderly nursing home patients. *The International Journal of Aging and Human Development, 51*(2), 137–141. https://doi.org/10.2190/5VY9-N1VT-VBFX-50RG

Fields, C. D. (2015). The loneliness of the Black Republican: Pragmatic politics and the pursuit of power. *Political Science Quarterly, 130*(4), 794–796. https://doi.org/10.1002/ polq.12427

Finkel, E. J., & Eastwick, P. W. (2008). Speed dating. *Association for Psychological Science, 17*(3), 193–197. https://doi.org/10.1111/j.1467-8721.2008.00573.x

Finkel, E. J., Eastwick, P. W., & Matthews, J. (2007). Speed-dating as an invaluable tool for chaptering romantic attraction: A methodological primer. *Personal Relationships, 14*, 149–166.

Fragnière, E., & Simon, M. (2019). Design de services et réseau d'acteurs Deux outils complémentaires pour une destination plus attractive. *Espaces*, 347, 10–11.

George, B. P., & Panko, T. R. (2011). Child sex tourism: Facilitating conditions, legal remedies, and other interventions. *Vulnerable Children and Youth Studies, 6*(2), 134–143.

George, R. (2021). *Marketing tourism and hospitality. Concepts and cases.* London: Palgrave.

Getz, D., & Page, S. J. (2020). *Theory, research, and policy for planned events.* London: Routledge.

Geurin-Eagleman, A. N., & Burch, L. M. (2016). Communicating via photographs: A gendered analysis of Olympic athletes' visual self-presentation on Instagram. *Sport Management Review, 19*(2), 133–145.

Gibson, C. (2012). Geographies of tourism: Space, ethics and encounter. In Wilson, J. (Ed.), *The Routledge handbook of tourism geographies* (pp. 72–77). Abingdon: Routledge.

Gilbert, D., Guerrier, Y., & Guy, J. (1998). Sexual harassment issues in the hospitality industry. *International Journal of Contemporary Hospitality Management, 10*(2), 48–53.

Gilbert, H. (1998). Responses to the sex trade: In post-colonial theatre. In Leigh, D., & Ryan, S. (Eds.), *The body in the library* (pp. 261–272). London: Brill.

Gladue, B. A., & Delaney, H. J. (1990). Gender differences in perception of attractiveness of men and women in bars. *Personality and Social Psychology Bulletin, 16*(2), 378–391. https://doi.org/10.1177/0146167290162017

Goodwin, C., & Lockshin, L. (1992). The solo consumer: Unique opportunity for the ServiceMarketer. *Journal of Services Marketing, 6*(3), 27–36.

Gravari-Barbas, M., & Graburn, N. (2016). *Tourism imaginaries at the disciplinary crossroads.* London: Routledge.

Gross, Z. (2018). Unpacking the landscape of female sex tourism in Kenya: A film analysis of paradise. *Love. Gender, Place & Culture, 25*(4), 507–524. https://doi.org /10.1080/0966369X.2018.1442816

Gunter, B. (2008). Internet dating: A British survey. *New Information Perspectives, 60*(2), 88–98.

Hanks, L., & Line, N. D. (2018). The restaurant social servicescape: Establishing a nomological framework. *International Journal of Hospitality Management, 74*, 13–21.

Harris, P. J., & Daley, J. (2008). Exploring the contribution of play to social capital in institutional adult learning settings. *Australian Journal of Adult Learning, 48*(1), 50–70.

Heimtun, B. (2012). The friend, the loner and the independent traveller: Norwegian midlife single women's social identities when on holiday. *Gender, Place & Culture, 19*(1), 83–101.

Heimtun, B., & Abelsen, B. (2013). Singles and solo travel: Gender and type of holiday. *Tourism Culture & Communication, 13*(3), 161–174.

Henderson, K. A., & Gibson, H. J. (2013). An integrative review of women, gender, and leisure: Increasing complexities. *Journal of Leisure Research, 45*(2), 115–135.

Heuser, L. (2004). We're not too old to play sports: The career of women lawn bowlers. *Leisure Studies, 24*(1), 45–60.

Hollenbaugh, E. E. (2021). Self-Presentation in social media: Review and Research Opportunities. *Review of Communication Research, 9*, 81–96.

Holst, J. (2017). The dynamic of play. Back to the basics of playing. *International Journal of Play, 6*(1), 85–95.

Hosseini, S., Macias, R. C., & Garcia, F. A. (2022). The exploration of Iranian solo female travellers' experiences. *International Journal of Tourism Research, 24*(2), 256–269. https://doi.org/10.1002/jtr.2498

Houser, M. L., Horan, S. M., & Furler, L. A. (2008). Dating in the fast lane: How communication predicts speed-dating success. *Journal of Social and Personal Relationships, 25*(5), 749–768.

https://www.tripadvisor.co.uk/Attraction_Review-g186338-d6153119-Reviews-Da teinaDash_Speed_Dating_Events-London_England.html

https://uk.trustpilot.com/review/dateinadash.com

Hudson, S., & Hudson, L. (2017). *Marketing for tourism, hospitality and events*. London: Sage.

Hutchinson, F. E. (2014). Malaysia's federal system: Overt and covert centralisation. *Journal of Contemporary Asia, 44*(3), 422–442.

Ibisworld. Dating Services in the UK - Market Research Report. Retrieved from https://www.ibisworld.com/united-kingdom/market-research-reports/dating-services-industry/, accessed on 28.11.22

Ingram, H. (2004). Sex and tourism: Journeys of romance, love and lust. *International Journal of Contemporary Hospitality Management, 16*(4), 273–274. https://doi.org/10.1108/09596110410537450

Islam, M. S., & Kirillova, K. (2020). Non-verbal communication in hospitality: At the intersection of religion and gender. *International Journal of Hospitality Management, 84*, 102326.

ITDR. (2020). *Solo travel: The growing trend in the coming years*. [online] ITDR.

Jacobs, J. (2009). Have sex will travel: Romantic 'sex tourism' and women negotiating modernity in the Sinai. *Gender Place & Culture, 16*(1), 43–61. https://doi.org/10.1080/09663690802574787

Jacobs, J. (2016). *Sex, tourism and the postcolonial encounter: Landscapes of longing in Egypt*. Abingdon: Routledge.

Jeffreys, S. (2003). Sex tourism: do women do it too?. *Leisure Studies, 22*(3), 223–238.

Johnson, M., & Barlow, R. (2021). Defining the phygital marketing advantage. *Journal of Theoretical and Applied Electronic Commerce Research, 16*, 2365–2385.

Jonas, L. C. (2022). Solo tourism: A great excuse to practice social distancing. *African Journal of Hospitality, Tourism and Leisure, 11*(SE1), 556–564.

Jordan, F., & Aitchison, C. (2008). Tourism and the sexualisation of the gaze: Solo female tourists' experiences of gendered power, surveillance and embodiment. *Leisure Studies, 27*(3), 329–349.

Karl, M. (2018). Risk and uncertainty in travel decision-making: Tourist and destination perspective. *Journal of Travel Research, 57*(1), 129–146.

Kerr, R., & Moore, K. (2015). Hard work or child's play? Migrant coaches's reflections on coaching gymnastics in New Zealand. *World Leisure Journal, 57*(3), 185–195.

Kesgin, M., Taheri, B., Murthy, R. S., Decker, J., & Gannon, M. J. (2021). Making memories: A consumer-based model of authenticity applied to living history sites. *International Journal of Contemporary Hospitality Management, 33*(10), 3610–3635.

Khalizadeh, J., & Pizam, A. (2021). Workplace romance across different industries with a focus on hospitality and leisure. *International Journal Hospitality Management.* https://doi.org/10.1016/j.ijhm.2020.102845

Kim, D. H., & Jang, S. C. (2017). Therapeutic benefits of dining out, traveling, and drinking: Coping strategies for lonely consumers to improve their mood. *International Journal of Hospitality Management, 67,* 106–114. https://doi.org/10.1016/j.ijhm.2017.08.013.

Kim, S.-H., Whaley, J. E., & Choi, Y. (2022). Managing the restaurant experience: Re-specifying the role of food interaction, and atmosphere as contributors to the optimal flow experience. *Journal of Foodservice Business Research.* https://doi.org/10.1080/15378020.2022.2047573

Klinenberg, E. (2013). *Going solo: The extraordinary rise and surprising appeal of living alone.* London: Penguin.

Korobov, N. (2011). Gendering desire in speed-dating interactions. *Discourse Studies, 13*(4), 461–485.

Korstanje, M. E. (2022). Failed hospitality: Human trafficking in the HBO Saga Westworld. In Korstanje, M. & Gowreesunkar, V. (Eds), *Handbook of research on present and future paradigms in human trafficking* (pp. 227–238). Hershey: IGI Global.

Korstanje, M. E., & Gowreesunkar, V. G. (Eds.). (2023). *Global perspectives on human rights and the impact of tourism consumption in the 21st century.* Hershey: IGI Global.

Korstanje, M. E., & Seraphin, H. (2022). A problem called alterity: The position of the 'other'in HBO Saga Westworld. In Korstanje, M.E., Seraphin, H., & Maingi, S. W. (Eds), *Tourism through troubled times: Challenges and opportunities of the tourism industry in the 21st century* (pp. 7–20). Bingley: Emerald Publishing Limited.

Kralj, A., & Solnet, D. (2010). Service climate and customer satisfaction in a casino hotel: An exploratory case chapter. *International Journal Hospitality Management, 29,* 711–719.

Lea, J. P. (1993). Tourism development ethics in the Third World. *Annals of Tourism Research, 20*(4), 701–715.

Lee, C. J., Wang, Y. C., & Cai, D. C. (2018). Physical factors to evaluate the servicescape of theme restaurants. *Journal of Asian Architecture and Building Engineering, 14*(1), 97–104.

Leeds-Hurwitz, W. (2015). Intercultural dialogue. In Tracy, C. I. K., & Sande, T. (Eds.), *International encyclopedia of language and social interaction* (vol. 2, pp. 860–868). Boston, MA: John Wiley & Sons.

Lehto, X. Y., Kirillova, K., Wang, D., & Fu, X. (2022). Convergence of boundaries in tourism, hospitality, events, and leisure: Defining the core and knowledge structure. *Journal of Hospitality & Tourism Research.* https://doi.org/10.1177/10963480221108667

Leith, C. (2020). Tourism trends: Lifestyle developments and the links to solo tourism. *Journal of Tourism Futures, 6*(3), 251–255.

Lewis, P. J. (2017). The erosion of play. *International Journal of Play, 6*(1), 10–23.

Li, F., He, C., & Qiao, G. (2021) Attributes that form romantic travel experience: A chapter of Chinese Generation Y tourists. *Current Issues in Tourism, 24*(15), 2130–2143.

Lin, I. Y. (2004). Evaluating a servicescape: The effect of cognition and emotion. *Hospitality Management, 23*, 163–178.

Lin, I. Y., & Mattila, A. S. (2010). Restaurant servicescape, service encounter, and perceived congruency on customers' emotions and satisfaction. *Journal of Hospitality Marketing & Management, 19*, 819–841.

Lu, T. S., Holmes, A., Noone, C., & Flaherty, G. T. (2020). Sun, sea and sex: A review of the sex tourism literature. *Tropical Diseases, Travel Medicine and Vaccines, 6*, 1–10.

Lub, X. D., Rijnders, R., Caceres, L. N., & Bosman, J. (2016). The future of hotels: The Lifestyle Hub. A design-thinking approach for developing future hospitality concepts. *Journal of Vocational Marketing, 22*(3), 249–264.

Lugosi, P. (2008). Hospitality spaces, hospitable moments: Consumer encounters and affective experiences in commercial settings. *Journal of foodservice, 19*, 139–149.

Mackinnon, L. (2022). Love, games and gamification: Gambling and gaming as techniques of modern romantic love. *Theory, Culture & Society, 39*(6), 121–137. https://doi.org/10.1177/02632764221078258

Manghani, S. (2017). The art of Paolo Cirio: exposing new myths of big data structures. *Theory, Culture & Society, 34*(7–8), 197–214.

Maximilian, B. (2019). From overtourism to sustainability: A research agenda for qualitative tourism development in the Adriatic. *MPRA*. Retrieved from https://mpra.ub.uni-muenchen.de/92213/

McKercher, B., & Bauer, T. G. (2003). The conceptual framework of the nexus between tourism, romance and sex. In Bauer, T. M., & McKercher, B. (Eds.), *Sex and tourism: Journeys of romance, love and lust* (pp. 3–16). Oxford: The Haworth Press.

McNamara, K. E., & Prideaux, B. (2010). A typology of solo independent women travellers. *International Journal of Tourism Research, 12*(3), 253–264.

Mele, C., & Russo-Spena, T. (2021). The architecture of the phygital customer journey: A dynamic interplay between systems of insights and systems of engagement. *European Journal of Marketing, 56*(1), 72–91

Montargot, N., Kallumuenzer, A., & Kraus, S. (2022). Haute cuisine three-star restaurants' representation on websites and dining guides: A lexicometric analysis. *International Journal of Contemporary Hospitality Management*. https://doi.org/10.1108/IJCHM-07-2021-0851

Moro, S., Batista, F., Rita, P., Oliveira, C. & Ribeiro, R. (2019). Are the states united? An analysis of US hotels' offers through TripAdvisor's eyes. *Journal of Hospitality & Tourism Research, 43*(7), 1112–1129.

Myers, K. (2016). Alice in transnational perspective and through the history of replication: An exploration of adult play in Australian art and Japanese shōjo culture. *International Journal of Play, 5*(3), 292–305.

Ngo, T., Hales, R., & Lohmann, G. (2019). Collaborative marketing for the sustainable development of community-based tourism enterprises: A reconciliation of diverse perspectives. *Current Issues in Tourism, 22*(18), 2266–2283.

Nomadher. Retrieved from https://www.nomadher.com

Nomadicyak. (2022). *Nomadicyak.* [online] Nomadicyak. Retrieved from https://www.nomadicyak.com/wp-content/uploads/2022/11/advantages-of-solo-travel.png, accessed on 21.03.24

O'Cass, A., & Sok, P. (2015). An exploratory study into managing value creation in tourism service firms: Understanding value creation phases at the intersection of the tourism service firm and their customers. *Tourism Management, 51*, 186–200.

O'Connell Davidson, J. (1996). Sex tourism in Cuba. *Race & Class, 38*(1), 39–48.

Okumus, F., Altinay, L., Chathoth, P., & Koseoglu, M. A. (2020). *Strategic management for hospitality and tourism.* London: Routledge.

Olds, K. (2007). Global assemblage: Singapore, foreign universities, and the construction of a 'global education hub'. *World Development, 35*(6), 959–975.

Olson, J. C., & Jacoby, J. (1972). Cue utilisation in the quality perception process. *Proceedings, Third Annual Conference of Association for Consumer Research,* 167–179.

Oppermann, M. (1999). Sex tourism. *Annals of Tourism Research, 26*(2), 251–266. https://doi.org/10.1016/S0160-7383(98)00081-4

O' Regan, M., Salazar, N. B., Choe, J., & Buhalis, D. (2022). Unpacking overtourism as a discursive formation through interdiscursivity. *Tourism Review, 77*(1), 54–71. https://doi.org/10.1108/TR-12-2020-0594

Orwell, G. (1989). *Nineteen eighty-four.* London: Penguin Books.

Panko, T. R., & George, B. P. (2012). Child sex tourism: Exploring the issues. *Criminal Justice Studies, 25*(1), 67–81.

Pearce, P. L., & Wu, M. Y. (2016). Tourists' evaluation of a romantic themed attraction: Expressive and instrumental issues. *Journal of Travel Research, 55*(2), 220–232.

Phillips, J. (2008). Female sex tourism in Barbados: A postcolonial perspective. *Brown Journal of World Affairs, 14,* 201.

Play Google. Retrieved from https://play.google.com/store/apps/details?id=com.nomadher.nomadher2&hl=en&gl=US

Poris, M. (2006). Understanding what fun means to today's kids. *Young Consumers, 7*(1), 14–22.

Powell, G. M., Cory, L., & Datillo, J. (2004). Opening the door: Social skills interventions as a facilitator of social play. *World Leisure Journal, 46*(3), 50.

Prince, S. (2017). Craft-art in the Danish countryside: Reconciling a lifestyle, livelihood and artistic career through rural tourism. *Journal of Tourism and Cultural Change, 15*(4), 339–358.

Quinn, B. (2013). *Key concepts in event management.* London: Sage.

Rasoolimanesh, S. M., Khoo-Lattimore, C., Md Noor, S., Jaafar, M., & Konar, R. (2021). Tourist engagement and loyalty: Gender matters? *Current Issues in Tourism, 24*(6), 871–885.

Redding, G. (2015). The thick description and comparison of societal systems of capitalism. *Journal of International Business Studies, 36,* 123–155.

Reimer, A., & Kuehn, R. (2004). The impact of servicescape on quality perception. *European Journal of Marketing, 39*(7/8), 785–808.

Resnick, M. (2004). Edutainment? No thanks. I prefer playful learning. Associazione Civita Report on Edutainment, 14. Retrieved September 20, 2019, from https://www.bibsonomy.org/bibtex/23c2f17d89ee28d884c9ff420cf25b68a/yish

Rivers-Moore, M. (2011). Imagining others: Sex, race, and power in transnational sex tourism. *ACME: An International Journal for Critical Geographies, 10*(3), 392–411.

Roman, L. (2021). *Why people solo travel: A pie chart of reasons to travel alone.* [online] WanderBIG.com. Retrieved from https://www.wanderbig.com/why-people-solo-travel/, accessed on 21.03.24

Rothenberg, A. (1996). The Janusian process in scientific creativity. *Creativity Research Journal, 9*(2), 207–231.

Ruddick, P. (2012). Dating contributes over £1bn to hospitality industry. BigHospitality. Retrieved from https://www.bighospitality.co.uk/Article/2012/01/26/Dating-contributes-over-1bn-to-hospitality-industry, accessed on 31.03.24

Rui, J., & Stefanone, M. A. (2013). Strategic self-presentation online: A cross-cultural chapter. *Computers in Human Behaviour, 29*, 110–118.

Ryan, C., & Kinder, R. (1996). Sex, tourism and sex tourism: Fulfilling similar needs? *Tourism Management, 17*(7), 507–518.

Sanchez de Rojas, I. M. (2020). *Solo travel: Extraordinary experiences and personal transformation* (Doctoral dissertation). Brasil. Fundacion Getulio Vargas (FGV).

Sanchez, P. M., & Adams, K. M. (2008). The Janus-faced character of tourism in Cuba. *Annals of Tourism Research, 35*(1), 27–46.

Scott, D., & Godbey, G. C. (1992). An analysis of adult play groups: Social versus serious participation in contract bridge. *Leisure Sciences, 14*, 47–67.

Seepersad, S., Choi, M. K., & Shin, N. (2008). How does culture influence the degree of romantic loneliness and closeness? *The Journal of Psychology, 142*(2), 209–220. https://doi.org/10.3200/JRLP.142.2.209-220

Seow, D., & Brown, L. (2020). The solo female Asian tourist. In Cooper, C., & Hall, M. (Eds.), *Current issues in Asian tourism* (pp. 36–54). Abingdon: Routledge.

Séraphin, H. (2021). COVID-19: An opportunity to review existing grounded theories in event studies, *Journal of Convention and Event Tourism, 22*(1), 3–35.

Séraphin, H. (2023). Speed dating events: Introducing 'Special interest and meso-adultainment events' as a new type of event to existing literature. *Journal of Convention & Events*. https://doi.org/10.1080/15470148.2023.2209341

Séraphin, H., & Chaney, D. (2024). Identifying and Understanding the Intersectional Cues that Matter for Customers in Speed Dating Events. *Event Management*, ahead of print, DOI https://doi.org/10.3727/152599524X17066809545647

Séraphin, H., Gowreesunkar, V., Zaman, M., & Bourliataux, S. (2019). Community based festivals as a tool to tackle tourismphobia and antitourism movements. *Journal of Hospitality and Tourism Management, 39*, 219–223.

Séraphin, H., & Yallop, A. (2023a). The marriage à la mode: Hospitality industry's connection to the dating services industry. *Hospitality Insights, 7*(1), 7–9.

Shen, X., Chick, G., & Pitas, N. A. (2017). From playful parents to adaptable children: A structural equation model of the relationships between playfulness and adaptability among young adults and their parents. *International Journal of Play, 6*(3), 244–254.

Singh, M., & Jackson, M. (2015). Online Dating Sites: A tool for romance scams or a lucrative e-business model?. *BLED 2015 Proceedings*. Available at https://aisel.aisnet.org/bled2015/8/

Sloan, P., Legrand, W., & Chen, J. S. (2013). *Sustainability in the hospitality industry. Principles of sustainable operations*. London: Routledge.

Solo Traveler World. (2023). *Solo Travel Statistics, Data 2023–2024: Historical Trends, Sources Cited*. [online] Retrieved from https://solotravelerworld.com/about/solo-travel-statistics-data/#:~:text=46%25%20of%20respondents%20travel%20three%20or%20more%20times%20per%20year.&text=24%25%20of%20readers%20spend%20more,planning%206%20months%20before%20departure, accessed on 21.03.24.

Solo Traveler World. (2024). *Solo Travel Statistics, Data 2023–2024: Historical Trends, Sources Cited*. [online] Solotravelerworld. Retrieved from https://solotravelerworld.

com/wp-content/uploads/2018/12/Screen-Shot-2018-12-06-at-10.45.28-AM.png, accessed on 21.03.24.

Song, H., Altinay, L., Sun, N., & Wang, L. (2018). The influence of social interactions on senior customers' experiences and loneliness. *International Journal of Contemporary Hospitality Management, 30*(8), 2773–2790.

Sousa, B., Malheiro, A., Liberato, D., & Liberato, P. (2021). Movie tourism and attracting new tourists in the post-pandemic period: A niche marketing perspective. In *Advances in tourism, technology and systems: Selected papers from ICOTTS20* (Vol. 1, pp. 373–384). Singapore: Springer.

SpeedDater. Retrieved from https://www.speeddater.co.uk/, accessed on 30.06.22

Statista (2023). Online Dating - United Kingdom. Retrieved from https://www.statista. com/outlook/dmo/eservices/dating-services/online-dating/united-kingdom

Stokoe, E. (2010). "Have you been married, or …?": Eliciting and accounting for relationship histories in speed-dating interaction. *Research on Language and Social Interaction, 43*(3), 260–282.

Tagg, B., & Wang, S. (2016). Globalisation, commercialisation, and learning to play at KidZania Kuala Lumpur. *International Journal of Play, 5*(2), 141–158.

Taylor, J. S. (2000). Tourism and 'embodied' commodities: Sex tourism in the Caribbean. In Clift, S. & Carter, S. (Eds.), *Tourism and sex: culture, commerce and coercion* (pp. 41–53). Leicester: Pinter.

Terziyska, I. (2021). Solo female travellers: The underlying motivation. In *Gender and tourism: Challenges and entrepreneurial opportunities* (pp. 113–127). Bingley: Emerald Publishing Limited.

Timmermans, E., & Alexopoulos, C. (2020). Anxiously searching for love (among other things): Attachment orientation and mobile dating application users' motives and outcomes. *Cyberpsychology, Behavior, and Social Networking, 23*(7), 447–452.

Tranter, B. (2010). Environmental activists and non-active environmentalists in Australi. *Environmental Politics, 19*(3), 413–429.

Tubadji, A. (2023). You'll never walk alone: Loneliness, religion, and politico-economic transformation. *Politics & Policy.* https://doi.org/10.1111/polp.12538

Turley, E. L., Monro, S., & King, N. (2017). Adventures of pleasure: Conceptualising consensual bondage, discipline, dominance and submission, and sadism and masochism as a form of adult play. *International Journal of Play, 6*(3), 324–334.

Turowetz, J., & Hollander, M. H. (2012). Assessing the experience of speed dating. *Discourse Studies, 14*(5), 635–658.

Van As, B. A. L., Imbimbo, E., Franceschi, A., Menesini, E., & Nocentini, A. (2022). The longitudinal association between loneliness and depressive symptoms in the elderly: A systematic review. *International Psychogeriatrics, 34*(7), 657–669. https://doi.org/10.1017/S1041610221000399

Van Vleet, M., & Feeney, B. (2015). Play Behavior and playfulness in adulthood. *Social and Personality Psychology Compass, 9*(11), 630–643.

Voogt, A. D. (2017). Strategic games in society: The geography of adult play. *International Journal of Play, 6*(3), 308–318.

Vo Thanh, T., Seraphin, H., Okumus, F., & Koseoglu, M. A. (2020). Organisational ambidexterity in tourism research: A systematic review. *Tourism Analysis, 25*(1), 137–152.

Wang, H., Jha, S., Livny, M., & McDaniel, P. D. (2004). Security policy reconciliation in distributed computing environments. 5th International Workshop on policies for Distributed Systems and Networks.

Wang, H. J., & Wu, C. H. (2020, April). Research and Design for Hotel Security Experience for Women Traveling Alone. In *IOP Conference Series: Materials Science and Engineering* (Vol. 825, No. 1, p. 012022). IOP Publishing.

Wilson, E., Holdsworth, L., & Witsel, M. (2009). Gutsy women? Conflicting discourses in women's travel guidebooks. *Tourism Recreation Research, 34*(1), 3–11.

Yang, E. C. L., Khoo-Lattimore, C., & Arcodia, C. (2017). A systematic literature review of risk and gender research in tourism. *Tourism Management, 58*, 89–100.

Yang, E. C. L., Yang, M. J. H., & Khoo-Lattimore, C. (2019). The meanings of solo travel for Asian women. *Tourism Review, 74*(5), 1047–1057.

Yang, J., Zhang, D., Liu, X., Li, Z., & Liang, Y. (2022). Reflecting the convergence or divergence of Chinese outbound solo travellers based on the stimulus-organism-response model: A gender comparison perspective. *Tourism Management Perspectives, 43*, 100982.

Yang, M. J. H., Khoo, C., & Yang, E. C. L. (2024). Exploring host-children's engagement in tourism: Transcending the dichotomy of universalism and cultural relativism. *Tourism Management, 100*, 104838.

Yi, S., Li, X., & Jai, T. M. (2018). Hotel guests' perception of best green practices: A content analysis of online reviews. *Tourism and Hospitality Research, 18*(2), 191–202.

Yu, X., Li, X., & Jai, T. M. (2017). The impact of green experience on customer satisfaction: Evidence from TripAdvisor. *International Journal of Contemporary Hospitality Management, 29*(5), 1340–1361.

Zacher, H., & Froidevaux, A. (2021). Life stage, lifespan, and life course perspectives on vocational behavior and development: A theoretical framework, review, and research agenda. *Journal of Vocational Behavior, 126*, 103476.

Zeng, G., De Vries, H. J., & Go, F. M. (2019). *Restaurant chains in China. The dilemma of standardisation versus authenticity.* London: Palgrave.

3 The Meta Dimension of Tourism and Hospitality

3.1 Overview

This study contributes to the field of tourism and hospitality literature through highlighting the existence of five distinct levels within the domain of hospitality, thereby expanding the conceptual framework in this area by including an additional level, while also applying it to the tourism industry. In line with the research findings, the Tasci and Semrad hospitality model would have to be updated to include a fifth 'meta-service' level.

The 'meta-service' layer of tourism and hospitality will look at meeting needs of customer which are related to societal issues from both a romantic perspective and an old-age perspective. It aligns with the current trend towards interdisciplinary studies within the academic landscape, a shift away from the isolation of research within specific disciplinaries. We draw upon the concept of 'atmospheric justice' to argue that the development and transformation of atmospheres should be a democratic process, involving collaboration between venues, employees, and customers. Speed dating is therefore a co-created event among three main stakeholders: the dating industry, the hospitality industry and the participants (co-creators of the experience). As for the tourism industry, it could play a role in the romantic of individual through apps such as TravelBuddy, *Nomadher*, etc. As a result, speed-dating and dating apps offer highly promising avenues for investigating the dynamics of initial romantic attraction and the early stages of relationship development.

The tourism and hospitality industries are playing a role in the contextual changes across the lifespan of individuals, which includes the periods: transition from school to work; career transition and finally transition from work to retirement (Zacher & Froidevaux, 2021). For the period 'transition from school to work', the hospitality industry offers many trainings, internships, career opportunities (Kusluvan, Akova & Kusluvan, 2022). For the period career transition, the industry has for a long time been a job provider for many (Aslan, 2016; Khalizadeh & Pizam, 2021). The tourism and hospitality industries are also playing a role in person change across the lifespan. It offers opportunities for people to celebrate joyful occasions such as weddings and

DOI: 10.4324/9781003502975-3

jubilees (Lau & Hui, 2010), and even commemorate sad events such as funerals (Filimonau & Brown, 2018).

The number of academic publications within the tourism and hospitality field that delve into intimate interactions among individuals is notably limited. These publications tend to focus on sex tourism (see part 2), or on specific range of topics, including instances of deviant sexual behaviour, such as sexual harassment among industry employees (Gilbert, Guerrier & Guy, 1998). Additionally, some research investigated emerging trends, such as the utilisation of motels or love motel hotels by couples for sexual encounters (Alexander et al., 2010; Ingram, 2004). In that sense, there is a focus on exploring romantic relationships and sexual encounters within these industries, whether among employees themselves or between industry personnel and tourists or customers (Aslan, 2016; Khalizadeh & Pizam, 2021). The existence of these publications underscores the importance and urgency of further research in this domain (Tews, Michel & Allen, 2014).

The purpose of this chapter is to advance practical and conceptual understanding of the relationship between business and society, and more specifically the ergonomic fitness of some businesses and industries to meet the needs of individuals in a constantly evolving society, where individuals sometimes experience limitations in achieving some of their objectives. Businesses in the technology sector, for instance, are often acknowledged for their ability to enhance human capabilities in many areas, whether professional (Upasani et al., 2023; Yang et al., 2023) or personal, including helping them in their romantic life (Blackwell, Birnholtz & Abbot, 2015). This study investigates the fitness of the hospitality industry, bars and restaurants in particular, to meet the changing practice of individuals in many Western societies when it comes to encountering and dating (Haywood, 2018) either during holidays or during the working period. This study is of importance because loneliness is a major societal issue (Sexton, 2022), mainly investigated and discussed from Old Age Pensioners (OAPs) perspective (Chatty Café Scheme, 2023 [Online]). The romantic aspect is totally overlooked and yet, the number of single individuals, and single households in the world is increasing (Statista, 2023). Same for the solo-travellers segment, whom sometimes happen to be single (Bente & Birgit, 2013).

This study is positioned at the intersection of business and society and thus finds itself within the literature related to corporate social performance (CSP) and corporate social responsibility (CSR). Indeed, corporate social performance and corporate social responsibility address the ways firms respond to societal expectations and help to evaluate to what extent they have met, exceeded or unmet the expectations (Griffin, 2000; Shabana, Buchholtz & Carroll, 2017). At the moment, the concepts remain quite corporate centric. When it comes to CSP and CSR, research essentially focuses first on organisations and their rules, processes and structures (Rothenberg, Hull & Tang, 2012; Shabana, Buchholtz & Carroll, 2017; Stites & Michael, 2011). Second, the wider economy and society, including the global economy, capitalism and related modes of production and consumption (Muller, 2020; Shabana, Buchholtz & Carroll, 2017; Orlitzky, Swanson & Quartermaine, 2006). Immediate relationships between people remain quasi-researched, and yet, relationships between individuals and the level of fun they have, play a role in the performance of an organisation and the level of happiness of individuals and their attachment to the organisation (Tews, Michel & Allen, 2014).

The exploration of contemporary dating as a consumptive act within market relations has established a certain level of connection with the service industries, and particularly the tourism industry. Haywood (2018) argues that holidays and romance are compatible, as holidays are fostering disinhibition and relationship acceleration. The present study is the first one discussing the fitness of the tourism and hospitality industry industries in terms of meeting the needs of individuals within societies for encountering and dating. Speed dating events are used in this study to explore a bigger topic of the role that the hospitality industry plays in the non-work interface of the life of individuals which includes finding a partner, having children and becoming parents (Zacher & Froidevaux, 2021). The non-work interface of the life of individuals is a major societal bone of contention and discussion (Carter & Duncan, 2018; Haywood, 2018; Olson & Fowers, 1993; Sassler & Lichter, 2020), because of some social conventions (Maillochon, 2012) around questions such as getting married, who to marry, at what age, etc. (Choi, 2019; Sassler & Lichter, 2020).

The study argues that the role of the tourism and hospitality industry in the non-work interface life of individuals is unsaturated, and much more can be done by the industry to make a more noticeable contribution. The concept of 'unsaturated contribution' is proposed and developed in this study and presents its first main contribution.

The second main contribution of the study is in suggesting that to fully meet the non-work interface needs of the present society, the four layers of hospitality (sustenance, entertainment, service, hospitableness) suggested by Tasci and Semrad (2016) that we are also applying to tourism, need to be reconsidered. More specifically, the study suggests the addition of a 'meta-service' layer which will focus on the non-work interface life of individuals.

3.2   Corporate Social Performance (CSP), and Corporate Social Responsibility (CSR) of the Tourism Hospitality Industries

According to Tasci and Semrad (2016), there is a noticeable absence of scholarly research that comprehensively explores all four levels of hospitality, which include the sustenance layer, which pertains to fulfilling the fundamental needs of customers, such as food and drink; the entertainment aspect, which caters to higher-level customer needs; the service dimension, involving the attentive fulfilment of needs through specific tasks; and hospitableness, characterised by the provision of care with a hospitable touch. Additionally, there is a lack of investigation into intimate interactions among customers within this framework. To address this critical gap in the existing literature, this study focuses on speed dating events as a contextual underpinning. Speed dating serves as a loose connection that can be strengthened through subsequent dates, leading potentially to the creation of a family. In essence, speed dating events can be viewed as a fundamental component of life-course linking.

The study by Séraphin and Yallop (2023a, 2023b) explores the unique intersection of the dating and hospitality industries through speed dating events. Speed dating events, organised by dating industry professionals and hosted in hospitality establishments such as bars and restaurants, have been subject to extensive academic scrutiny (Berrios, Totterdell & Niven, 2015; Finkel, Eastwick & Matthews, 2007; Fisman et al., 2006; Hollander & Turowetz, 2013; Kadlec, 2019; Kulbe, 2014). This body of research explores various aspects of speed dating events, encompassing factors influencing attraction between participants (Finkel, Eastwick & Matthews, 2007), gender-based differences in partner selection (Fisman et al., 2006), the emotional experiences of attendees (Berrios et al., 2015), motivations for participating in speed dating events (Turowetz & Hollander, 2012; Hollander & Turowetz, 2013), teaching approaches related to gender theory (Sweet, 2015), technological advancements in the context of speed dating (Kadlec, 2019), and the determinants of successful 'matches' at these events (Kulbe, 2014). This extensive research demonstrates the multifaceted nature of speed dating events and their significance in both the dating and hospitality industries.

For example, Finkel, Eastwick and Matthews (2007) argue that speed dating offers an approach for examining the dynamics of initial romantic attraction and the early stages of relationship formation. In that sense, Berscheid and Regan (2005) stated that

> to understand why others currently are in the relationships they are—and to understand why we ourselves developed the relationships we did—it is usually necessary to retrace the history of the relationship back to its very beginning and to identify the causal conditions that were in force at that time.

From a romantic human interaction perspective, Séraphin (2023) indicates that leveraging assets from both the dating and hospitality industries can enhance attraction and desire among speed daters. This can be achieved through the application of multisensory extended reality technologies, which engage all five human senses (vision, touch, hearing, taste, and smell). Indeed, multisensory extended reality, which is a form of technology which uses human five senses i.e., 'vision (HMD, 360° videos), touch (haptic gloves, mid-air haptics), hearing (headsets), taste (electronic tongue) and smell (olfactory and diffuser technology, electronic nose)' (Santoso, Wang & Windasari, 2022: 357). The study also raises questions about the role of venue design in shaping the dynamics of speed dating events. It explores whether the venue's design affirms or disaffirms the close relationship between design and successful matchmaking during the event.

In line with Michelangelo Model which suggests that 'close partners sculpt one another's selves, shaping one another's skills and traits and promoting versus inhibiting one another's goal pursuits' (Rusbult, Finkel & Kumashiro, 2009). The model also suggests that close partners play a role in 'affirming versus disaffirming one another's pursuit of the ideal self' (Kumashiro et al., 2007). The hospitality industry is either helping individuals attending speed dating events to affirm or disaffirm themselves with regards to their pursuit of their soulmate. What role does the design of the venue (hospitality industry) play in this pursuit? Is it affirming or disaffirming the contribution of the hospitality industry in the romantic life of individuals.

As opposed to existing research that explores individual determinants influencing 'match' outcomes at speed dating events, this study shifts its focus towards extrinsic factors. Specifically, it investigates the role of the space and design of bars and restaurants in contributing to the success, characterised by participant 'matching', in speed dating events. Existing research on human relationships, particularly at such intimate activities as dating, the influence of the hospitality industry environment, including bars and restaurants, has been overlooked.

Nevertheless, existing research in the field of hospitality highlights the significance of the environment, including interior design, in shaping consumer behaviour, as exemplified by factors influencing booking decisions (Nanu et al., 2020). Moreover, the interior colour schemes of hospitality venues have been shown to evoke emotions in customers, thus impacting their choices regarding venue selection (Tantanatewin & Inkarojrit, 2018). The design of hospitality spaces has demonstrated a direct effect on customer well-being when tailored to their needs (Lee, 2020), as well as an indirect influence when designed to accommodate their pets (Buhalis & Chan, 2023). Finally, within the hospitality context, research grounded in the Stimulus-Organisation-Response (S.O.R) framework has established a profound connection between hospitableness, customer experiences, emotions, satisfaction, subjective well-being, and a positive perception of the organisation (Altinay et al., 2023). The context and the environment are also very important in tourism when it comes to wedding tourism, for instance. Indeed, some destinations thanks to their environment have developed over the years an image of romantic destination, case (Bertella, 2015, 2016).

Following these lines of thought, our study contributes to the body of knowledge in three ways:

First, in considering the four distinct levels within the context of hospitality presented by Tasci and Semrad (2016), this study contributes to the field of tourism and hospitality literature through highlighting the existence of five distinct levels, thereby expanding the conceptual framework in this area by including an additional level.

Second, the study adopts a distinctive approach by directing its focus towards the social dimension of the tourism and hospitality industry. This shift from the traditional emphasis on business and operational aspects, as often found in prior research (Bowie et al., 2017; George, 2021; Hudson & Hudson, 2017; Okumus et al., 2020), aligns with the emerging call for further exploration of the social facets within the field. The tourism industry plays a role in many aspects of our lives such as gap year through activities such as volunteering tourism (Lyons et al., 2012); the honeymoon after the wedding, which is to be related to wedding tourism (Bertella, 2015, 2016); some individuals are involved in sex tourism to meet some personal and physiologic needs (Opperman, 1999; Leheny, 1995); tourism is also using the transmission of values from the older members of the family to the youngest (Miyakawa & Oguchi, 2022; Xu & Kahl, 2018; Xu et al., 2022), etc. Altinay et al. (2023) have also stressed the necessity for further research into the social dimensions of the hospitality industry. While previous social research within hospitality has considered areas such as hospital patients (Altinay et al., 2023), healthcare in general (Pizam, 2022), the experience of loneliness among individuals (Kim & Jang, 2017), the experiences of migrants (Zopiatis, Constanti & Theocharous, 2014), among others, no studies have investigated loneliness through a romantic lens. Given the global prevalence of loneliness as a societal concern (Sexton, 2022), our study's examination of loneliness within the context of speed dating events is unique.

Third, this research aligns with the current trend towards interdisciplinary studies within the academic landscape, a shift away from the isolation of research within specific disciplinaries (Ziakas & Getz, 2020). This interdisciplinary orientation reflects a broader movement in business management, where products and services are increasingly explored as portfolios rather than individual entities (Ziakas, 2019). The strategic advantages of this approach draw upon the integration and synergy among products, services and the stakeholders involved (Ziakas, 2019; Antchak, Ziakas & Getz, 2019). This strategy also has the potential to ease tensions and disparities related to values, approaches and other factors among involved parties (Ziakas & Costa, 2011). However, the comprehensive and sustainable management of portfolios encounters resistance due to the entrenched tradition of investigating industries and disciplines in isolation (Ziakas & Getz, 2020). This divergence from an integrated approach impedes the sustainable development of industries and disciplines (Antchak et al., 2019), often due to conflicting interests among these entities (Van Niekerk & Getz, 2019). Our study thus aligns with the call for greater interdisciplinary collaboration and integration within the academic and industry landscape, fostering a more holistic approach to research and development.

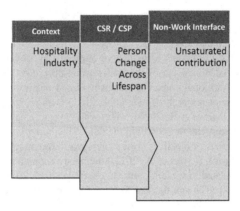

Figure 3.1 The tourism and hospitality industry and its social role.

The tourism and hospitality industries are playing a role in the contextual and person changes across the lifespan of individuals. As proven by existing research, notably on intimate relationship among individuals (sexual and/or romantic), the involvement of the hospitality industry is notably limited. The tourism and hospitality industry are performing their social role (Figure 3.1). However, from a performance perspective, CSP and CSR could be expanded, hence our claim that the contribution of the tourism and hospitality industries to the life of their consumers is 'unsaturated'. In other words, the tourism and hospitality industry can further contribute to the life of individuals. Hence also the reason we are suggesting another layer should be added to the Tasci and Semrad (2016) model.

Figure 3.2 indicates the additional layer we are suggesting adding to Tasci and Semrad (2016) model.

As we extend the Tasci and Semrad (2016) hospitality model to incorporate this new dimension, several avenues for future research emerge, contributing to the evolving landscape of interdisciplinary studies and societal engagement. The following directions outline potential areas for further exploration. A potential future research direction, scholars are encouraged to explore variations in the 'meta-service' level across cultural and geographical contexts to understand its nuanced manifestations investigating the societal impact of the 'meta-service' layer, focusing on how hospitality practices contribute to addressing societal issues, especially from romantic and old-age perspectives. Future research approaches can include examining the role of technology in enhancing and optimising the delivery of 'meta-services' within the tourism and hospitality industry exploring cross-industry collaborations to enhance the understanding and implementation of this 'meta-service' level. Embracing an interdisciplinary approach will be crucial in navigating the complexities of the 'meta-service' layer and its integration into the broader service industry.

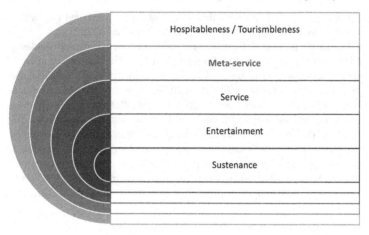

Figure 3.2 New layers of tourism and hospitality.

3.3 Research Avenues

3.3.1 Atmosphere

A recently published paper by Rokka et al. (2023) entitled *'Dynamics of Convivial Atmospheres'* highlighted how important compelling convivial atmospheres are for customers' experience, the competitive advantages of businesses, and their long-term sustainability. The authors used Club Med, a notoriously known resort for its convivial atmosphere as a case study. The article provides an excellent overview of how Club has built its image and reputation on this convivial atmosphere. Other recently published articles have also highlighted the importance of convivial atmospheres in service industries such as tourism (Paiva, 2023) and the event industry (Rosetti, 2023).

Additionally, in their research Rokka et al. (2023) also highlighted how challenging it is for service providers and their staff to create and maintain a convivial atmosphere, because it is an intangible competitive advantage partly co-created with customers and their affective capacities. The latter need to be willing to affect and be affected. The model of convivial atmosphere developed by Club Med is based on rituals (such as employees and customers eating together), and specific attitudes i.e., playfulness, liveliness, social interactions, togetherness, fun activities, etc., are key (Rokka et al., 2023).

Speed dating events, playful moments for adults, which foster social interactions among attendees (Alexopoulos et al., 2020), in an inclusive (Finkel & Eastwick, 2008; Turowetz & Hollander, 2012), hospitality environment, which can be either bars or restaurants (Séraphin, 2023) are also based on rituals and specific attitude. In both cases, success depends on the willingness of participants to fully immerse themselves into the context, and willingness to be affected by others (Luo & Zhang, 2009; Rokka et al., 2023).

Despite the previously discussed similarities between the hospitality industry and the dating services with regard to atmosphere, it also remains an area of divergence in terms of investigation. Indeed, in hospitality, criteria for convivial and non-convivial atmosphere (Rokka et al., 2023); atmospheric justice and atmospheric injustice (Paiva, 2023) are investigated from different perspectives which include tradition and socio-cultural perspectives; community engagement; experience; etc. (Paiva, 2023). Atmosphere at speed dating events are only discussed from the perspective of factors contributing to matching, which are themselves only discussed from a physiological, physical, and communication perspectives (Alexopoulos et al., 2020; Bhargava & Fisman, 2014; Finkel & Eastwick, 2008; Houser et al., 2008; Ranganath et al., 2009; Turowetz & Hollander, 2012).

3.3.2   Gaps in Literature

Academic research in personality and social psychology does not consider hospitality venues as a dimension that plays a role in dates and dating. Indeed, the only two publications in personality and social psychology which are considering hospitality venues and customer to customer (C2C) interactions, are exclusively focusing on bars, to explain that both, the quantity of alcohol consumed, and the time in the evening are variable impacting on perception of attractiveness (Gladue & Delaney, 1990). Despite the fact these publications are not about dates and dating, they both acknowledge bars as natural laboratory to explore romantic interactions among individuals (Gladue & Delaney, 1990; Sprecher et al., 1984). Having said that, not considering bars and restaurants when investigating the topics of dates and dating is a major gap in literature since the hospitality contexts, and particularly bars and restaurants are playing a major role in the social life of consumers (Yeoman, 2013). Equally important, it is to note that speed dating events are hosted by hospitality venues such as bars and restaurants (Séraphin, 2023; Séraphin & Yallop, 2023).

Hospitality academic research does not really explore the topic of romance and attraction. The only articles found on the topic only mention the fact that hospitality settings offer suitable context for romantic encounters, for both customers (Ingram, 2004) and staff (Khalizadeh & Pizam, 2021; Pizam, 2016). In the hospitality industry, being branded as a romantic venue is quite important for businesses (particularly restaurants) since every year you have the ranking of most romantic restaurants (architecturaldigest.com [Online]; enjoytravel.com [Online]). These restaurants are perceived as romantic because of the (1) Entertainment. Chefs and their food are often considered as part of the entertainment. (2) Décor. They often have chandeliers, candlelight, flowers, etc. (3) The lighting systems. Chandeliers, candles, and lanterns are often used. (4) Special effects. In the case of restaurants, the special effects are created by the food and drinks. French and Italian food and setting are particularly romantic. These four elements are important in terms of delivering memorable special events (Matthews, 2008), particularly when it comes to events such as weddings (Daniels & Loveless, 2007; Haverly, 2022).

Academic research in personality and social psychology does not consider at all event management from an operation perspective as a dimension that plays a role in dates and dating, and yet, there is a wide range of publications on speed dating events (Chang et al., 2020; Fisman et al., 2006; McClure et al., 2010; Wu et al., 2022). Having said that, not considering event management when investigating the topics of dates and dating is a major gap in literature since speed dating events are a type of event, coined by Séraphin (2023) as special interest adult entertainment (adultainment) events.

Servicescape, or the design of an environment is a form of communication, that sends stimuli to consumers who interpret them mentally and physically, before engaging with them (Berridge, 2007). As such, servicescape plays a central role in the experience of consumers (Berridge, 2007). This makes the choice of venue extremely important, as it plays a role on the type of stimuli sent to participants, and their level of engagement (Daniels & Loveless, 2007; Haverly, 2022; Matthews, 2008). Venue management, which includes décor, lighting, audio, entertainment, etc., is an important aspect of event management (Matthews, 2008). Research in personality and social psychology can help event management research to explore and understand dimensions of customer service of groups so far unknown to the industry, such as speed daters, and tap into markets such as dating services.

Finally, research in tourism has also been totally overlooked by personality and social psychology, and yet, sex tourism is a rather well research topic of research (Herold et al., 2001; Opperman, 1999). The topic of sex tourism is also to be related to the hospitality industry, as restaurants, hotels, brothels (Herold et al., 2001; Leheny, 1995), bars such as Gogo-bars, topless-bars are often places of encounters (Opperman, 1999; Leheny, 1995). Research in personality and social psychology, and specifically on speed dating can play a transformative role for the tourism industry, helping some destinations to switch from sex tourism to 'romantic encounter tourism'. Tackling sex tourism through hospitality or event management related strategies has not been investigated and discussed so far in academic research. Instead, it has been for instance suggested legal routes (Bystrzanowski & Aramberri, 2003), or linguistic options such as abandoning the value laden term 'sex tourism' (Carr, 2016), etc. Therefore, future research could look at how the hospitality industry could work collaboratively with the tourism industry to address this issue.

3.3.3   Gap in Services

This chapter coins and defines the Economy of Romantic Loneliness (ERL) as the ecosystem gathering all the stakeholders providing and benefiting economically from products and services aiming at individuals who are looking for a romantic relationship, and equally important, in other words, individual looking to put an end of their romantic loneliness. The dating industry through dating apps and speed dating events seem to be the main actor of the ERL. The hospitality and tourism industry are not presenting themselves as actors of the ERL, and yet, they have a card to play in this economy. From a social point of view, they can contribute to address both good health and wellbeing (SDG 3) and economic growth (SDG 8). To address these SDGs, the tourism and hospitality industries will have to develop products and services dedicated to the 'single' members of the society, and/or improve some existing products and services so that they fully meet the needs of the single. From a tourism management perspective for instance, destinations that are known to be sex tourism destinations, could develop products and services more geared at facilitating romantic encounters (and not sexual encounters) for solo travellers for instance. This form of tourism could be branded as 'Romantic Encounter Tourism' (RET), and the destinations branded as 'Romantic Encounter Destinations' (RED). Practically, this means that bars such as Gogo-bars, topless-bars which are often places of encounters for sex (Opperman, 1999; Leheny, 1995), would be replaced by venues offering events where solo travellers who are single and looking for romance could meet solo travellers with the same profile and needs. This would help these destinations to move away the negative image of sex tourism (Herold et al., 2001; Ingram, 2004; Leheny, 1995; Opperman, 1999).

3.3.4   Research Agenda

3.3.4.1   Overview

By investigating date and dating through the hospitality prism, this chapter is enabling the understanding on a specific type of human interaction through a type of service provided. Speed dating events fall under the hospitableness layer of the hospitality industry since this type of event is related to heart-warming, heart assuring, and heart soothing service (Tasci & Semrad, 2016). By investigating date and dating through the event management prism, this chapter is enabling the understanding on a specific type of human interaction through the prism of atmospheric and how the operation side of event management contribute to the creation of this atmosphere. The concept of atmospheric is indeed quite central to service industries such as hospitality (Rokka et al., 2023) and event management (Rosetti, 2023).

Aesthetic, sensuous and sensory stimulations are considered for providing optimum experience. Extensive definition of atmosphere, atmospheric design and management had led to in depth analyses with multidisciplinary approaches (Rokka et al., 2023). The application of Möbius strip in relation with the Consumer Culture Theory (CCT) demonstrates a link of such kind between event management and marketing (Coffin & Chatzidakis, 2021).

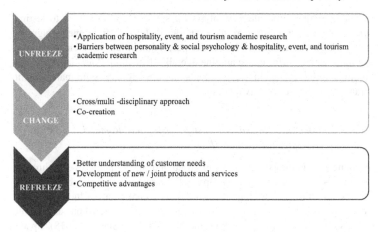

Figure 3.3 Model of cross/multi-disciplinary approach.

Furthermore, the Möbius strip as well-known mathematical object deployed by various academic fields even only as a metaphor outlines the connection with topology and its cultural dimension. The argument that topology allows the contemporary researchers to explore social formations, events and situations from everyday life (Shields, 2012) still exists in limited scope of debate. The literature provides evidence for the need of broad range methods and theoretical frameworks (Figure 3.3) to enrich the content of atmosphere (Coffin & Chatzidakis, 2021).

3.3.4.2 Speed Dating Events and Atmosphere

Using academic literature in hospitality management, i.e. hospitability setting (bars/restaurants), and event management (the execution of speed dating events, from a planning and delivering perspectives) future research should be looking at providing evidence that atmosphere is also a criterion that can be used to evaluate the success of speed dating events, as atmosphere plays a role in attraction and matching among individuals. This is important because at the moment, the level of physical attractions and matching among participants (Chang et al., 2020; Van der Meij et al., 2019; Wu et al., 2022) seem to be the only criteria used in existing literature to gauge the success of this type of event. Verbal and non-verbal communication is very often pointed out as central to attractiveness among individuals attending speed dating events (Bhargava & Fisman, 2014; Houser et al., 2008; Ranganath et al., 2009). The suggested future research should provide evidence that atmosphere (construct articulated around hospitality and event management) is also a form of communication that can contribute to match making.

Additionally, atmospheric analysis for speed dating can refer to testing and results of the atmosphere as a vital attribute of festival event (Nguyen et al., 2023). The attendees place/space perception influences their behaviour, communicative performance and the overall satisfaction. Potential study and findings of the settings for dating events may convey successful management strategies and post event evaluation.

3.3.4.3   'Romantic Atmospheric Justice' (RAJ) and 'Romantic Atmospheric Injustice' (RAI)

A connection is drawn between Club Med and Speed dating events through the famous French trilogy 'Les Bronzés', a satire of both Club Med style resorts, and middle-class tourists of the time, where many of the main characters found their partner, apart from Jean-Claude Dusse, whom despite all his effort to 'score' always fails to find his soulmate (Staszak, 2018). Speed dating events are based on the same principles. Participants either match or do not match with someone else at the end of the event (Finkel, Eastwick & Matthews, 2007).

This chapter is therefore suggesting future research to investigate the concepts of 'Romantic Atmospheric Justice' (RAJ) and 'Romantic Atmospheric Injustice' (RAI). To do so, future research could address the following research questions:

RQ1: How can the tourism and hospitality industry work together to develop 'Romantic Atmospheric Justice' (RAJ)?
RQ2: What is the economic potential of romantic tourism for a destination?

This chapter is not a mere criticism of academic research of existing research on personality and social psychology, and tourism, hospitality and event management. Rather, the purpose of this chapter is to bring the limitations of existing research to the attention of academics in that field. The chapter also provides suggestions for future research which should seek to explore the speed dating model through a variety of the prisms.

References

Alexander, M., Chen, C. C., MacLaren, A., & O'Gorman, K. D. (2010). Love motels: Oriental phenomenon or emergent sector? *International Journal Contemporary Hospitality Management, 22*(2), 194–208.
Alexopoulos, K., Nikolakis, N., & Chryssolouris, G. (2020). Digital twin-driven supervised machine learning for the development of artificial intelligence applications in manufacturing. *International Journal of Computer Integrated Manufacturing, 33*(5), 429–439.

Alexopoulos, C., Timmermans, E., & McNallie, J. (2020). Swiping more, committing less: Unravelling the links among dating app use, dating app success, and intention to commit infidelity. *Computers in Human Behaviour, 102,* 172–180.

Altinay, L., Alrawadieh, Z., Tulucu, F., & Arici, H. E. (2023). The effect of hospitableness on positive emotions, experience, and well-being of hospital patients. *International Journal Hospitality Management.* https://doi.org/10.1016/j.ijhm.2023.103431

Antchak, V., Ziakas, V., & Getz, D. (2019). *Event portfolio management: Theory and practice for event management and tourism.* Oxford: Goodfellow.

Aslan, A. (2016). An exploratory study on the sexual intimacy of male hotel workers and foreign female tourists. *International Journal Contemporary Hospitality Management.* https://doi.org/10.1016/j.ijhm.2016.08.003

Bente, H., & Birgit, A. (2013). Singles and solo travel: Gender and type of holiday. *Tourism Culture & Communication, 13*(3), 161–174.

Berrios, R., Totterdell, P., & Niven, K. (2015). Why do you make us feel good? Correlates and interpersonal consequences of affective presence in speed-dating. *European Journal of Personality, 29,* 72–82.

Berscheid, E., & Regan, P. (2005). *The psychology of interpersonal relationships.* New York: Prentice-Hall.

Bertella, G. (2015). Celebrating the family abroad: The wedding tourism experience. *Annals of Leisure Research, 18*(3), 397–413.

Bertella, G. (2016). The emergence of Tuscany as a wedding destination: The role of local wedding planners. *Tourism Planning & Development, 14*(1), 1–14.

Bhargava, S., & Fisman, R. (2014). Contrast effects in sequential decisions: Evidence from speed dating. *The Review of Economics and Statistics, 96*(3), 444–457.

Blackwell, C., Birnholtz, J., & Abbot, C. (2015). Seeing and being seen: Co-situation and impression formation using Grindr, a location-aware gay dating app. *New Media & Society, 17*(7), 1117–1136.

Bowie, D., Buttle, F., Brookes, M., & Mariussen, A. (2017). *Hospitality marketing.* Routledge.

Buhalis, D., & Chan, J. (2023). Traveling with pets: Designing hospitality services for pet owners/parents and hotel guests. *International Journal of Contemporary Hospitality Management.* https://doi.org/10.1108/IJCHM-10-2022-1192

Carter, J., & Duncan, S. (2018). *Individualised conformity: Creating a wedding. in: Reinventing couples.* Palgrave Macmillan Studies in Family and Intimate Life. London: Palgrave Macmillan.

Choi, K. H. (2019). Racial diversity in the marital assimilation of Hispanics. *Journal of Marriage and the Family, 82*(2), 675–690.

Coffin, J., & Chatzidakis, A. (2021). The Möbius strip of market spatiality: mobilizing transdisciplinary dialogues between CCT and the marketing mainstream. *AMS Review, 11,* 40–59. https://doi.org/10.1007/s13162-020-00191-8

Daniels, M., & Loveless, C. (2007). Wedding planning management. *Consultancy for diverse clients.* Routledge: London.

Filimonau, V., & Brown, L. (2018). 'Last hospitality' as an overlooked dimension in contemporary hospitality theory and practice. *International Journal of Contemporary Hospitality Management, 74,* 67–74.

Finkel, E. J., & Eastwick, P. W. (2008). Speed-dating. *Current Directions in Psychological Science, 17*(3), 193–197.

Finkel, E. J., Eastwick, P. W., & Matthews, J. (2007). Speed-dating as an invaluable tool for studying romantic attraction: A methodological primer. *Personal Relationships, 14*, 149–166.

Fisman, R., Iyengar, S. S., Kamenica, E., & Somonson, I. (2006). Gender differences in mate selection: Evidence from a speed dating experiment. *The Quarterly Journal of Economics, 121*(2), 673–697.

George, R. (2021). *Marketing tourism and hospitality. Concepts and cases.* London: Palgrave.

Gilbert, D., Guerrier, Y., & Guy, J. (1998). Sexual harassment issues in the hospitality industry. *International Journal of Contemporary Hospitality Management, 10*(2), 48–53.

Griffin, J. J. (2000). Corporate social performance: Research directions for the 21st century. *Business & Society, 39*(4), 479–491. https://doi.org/10.1177/000765030003900407

Hanks, L., & Line, N. D. (2018). The restaurant social servicescape: Establishing a nomological framework. *International Journal of Hospitality Management, 74*, 13–21.

Harris, P. J., & Daley, J. (2008). Exploring the contribution of play to social capital in institutional adult learning settings. *Australian Journal of Adult Learning, 48*(1), 50–70.

Haverly, M. (2022). *The practical guide to wedding planning.* Routledge: London.

Haywood, C. (2018). *Men, masculinity and contemporary dating.* London: Palgrave Macmillan.

Herold, E., Garcia, R., & DeMoya, T. (2001). Female tourists and beach boys: Romance or Sex Tourism? *Annals of Tourism Research, 28*(4), 978–997, doi: 10.1016/S0160-7383(01)00003-2.

Hill, C., Hegde, A. L., & Matthews, C. (2014). Throwing in the towel: Burnout among practicing interior designers. *Journal of Interior Design, 39*(3), 41–60. https://doi.org/10.1111/joid.12029

Hollander, M. M., & Turowetz, J. (2013). 'So, why did you decide to do this?' Soliciting and formulating motives for speed dating. *Discourse & Society.* https://doi.org/10.1177/0957926513503268

Houser, M. L., Horan, S. M. & Furler, L. A. (2008). Dating in the fast lane: How communication predicts speed-dating success. *Journal of Social and Personal Relationships, 25*(5), 749–768.

Hudson, S., & Hudson, L. (2017). *Marketing for tourism, hospitality and events.* London: Sage.

Ingram, H. (2004). Sex and tourism: Journeys of romance, love and lust. *International Journal Contemporary Hospitality Management, 16*(4), 273–274.

Kadlec, V. (2019). Speed dating: An effective tool for technology transfer in a fragmented regional innovation system? *AUC Geographica, 54*(1), 57–66.

Khalizadeh, J., & Pizam, A. (2021). Workplace romance across different industries with a focus on hospitality and leisure. *International Journal Hospitality Management.* https://doi.org/10.1016/j.ijhm.2020.102845

Kim, D. K., & Jang, S. (2017). Therapeutic benefits of dining out, traveling, and drinking: Coping strategies for lonely consumers to improve their mood. *International Journal of Hospitality Management, 67*, 106–114.

Kulbe, G. (2014). The effects of confidence on attractiveness, across online- and speed-dating contexts (Honours Thesis). School of Psychology, The University of Queensland.

Kumashiro, M., Rusbult, C., Finkenauer, C., & Stocker, S. L. (2007). To think or to do: The impact of assessment and locomotion orientation on the Michelangelo phenomenon. *Journal of Social and Personal Relationships, 24*(4), 591–611.

Kusluvan, H., Akova, O., & Kusluvan, S. (2022). Occupational stigma and career commitment: Testing mediation and moderation effects of occupational self-esteem. *International Journal Hospitality Management.* https://doi.org/10.1016/j.ijhm.2022.103149

Lau, C. K. H., & Hui, S. H. (2010). Selection attributes of wedding banquet venues: An exploratory study of Hong Kong prospective wedding couples. *International Journal Hospitality Management, 29*(2), 268–276.

Lee, S. (2020). Investigating the importance of positive hotel design. *International Journal Hospitality Management.* https://doi.org/10.1016/j.ijhm.2020.102523

Leheny, D. (1995). A political economy of Asian sex tourism. *Annals of Tourism Research, 22*(2), 367–384.

Line, N. D., Hanks, L., & McGinley, S. (2018). When birds flock together: An identification of the destination social servicescape. *Journal of Travel & Tourism Marketing, 35*(7), 882–894. https://doi.org/10.1080/10548408.2018.1445065.

Luo, S., & Zhang, G. (2009). What leads to romantic attraction: Similarity, reciprocity, security, or beauty? evidence from a speed-dating study. *Journal of Personality.* https://doi.org/10.1111/j.1467-6494.2009.00570.x

Lyons, K., Hanley, J., Wearing, S., & Neil, J. (2012). Gap year volunteer tourism: Myths of Global Citizenship? *Annals of Tourism Research, 39*(1), 361–378.

Maillochon, F. (2012). Le Coeur et la raison. Amis et parents invites au marriage. *Geneses, 83*(2), 93–117.

Matthews, D. (2008). *Special Event Production.* BH.

Miyakawa, E., & Oguchi, T. (2022). Family tourism improves parents' well-being and children's generic skills. *Tourism Management.* https://doi.org/10.1016/j.tourman.2021.104403

Muller, A. (2020). When does corporate social performance pay for international firms? *Business & Society, 59*(8), 1554–1588. https://doi.org/10.1177/0007650318816957

Nanu, L., Ali, F., Berezina, K., & Cobanoglu, C. (2020). The effect of hotel lobby design on booking intentions: An intergenerational examination. *International Journal Hospitality Management.* https://doi.org/10.1016/j.ijhm.2020.102530

Nguyen, G. T. H., Hoang-Cong, H., & La, L. T. (2023). Statistical analysis for understanding PM2. 5 air quality and the impacts of COVID-19 social distancing in several provinces and cities in Vietnam. *Water, Air, & Soil Pollution, 234*(2), 85.

Okumus, F., Altinay, L., Chathoth, P., & Koseoglu, M. A. (2020). *Strategic management for hospitality and tourism.* London: Routledge.

Olson, D. H., Fowers, B. J. (1993). Five types of marriage: An empirical typology based on ENRICH. *The Family Journal, 1*(3), 196–207.

Oppermann, M. (1999). Sex tourism. *Annals of Tourism Research, 26*(2), 251–266, doi: 10.1016/S0160-7383(98)00081-4.

Orlitzky, M., Swanson, D. L., & Quartermaine, L.-K. (2006). Normative myopia, executives' personality, and preference for pay dispersion: Toward implications for corporate social performance. *Business & Society, 45*(2), 149–177. https://doi.org/10.1177/0007650306286739

Paiva, D. (2023). The paradox of atmosphere: Tourism, heritage, and urban liveability. *Annals of Tourism Research, 101*, 103600. https://doi.org/10.1016/j.annals.2023.103600

Pizam, A. (2016). Workplace romance in the hospitality industry. *International Journal of Hospitality Management*, https://doi.org/10.1016/j.ijhm.2016.06.001

Pizam, A. (2022). The rationale for hospitability in healthcare. *International Journal of Hospitability Management*. https://doi.org/10.1016/j.ijhm.2022.103399

Ranganath, R., Jurafsky, D. & Farland, D. (2009). It's Not You, it's Me: Detecting Flirting and its Misperception in speed-dates. *Proceedings of the 2009 Conference on Empirical Methods in Natural Language Processing*, pp. 334–342, Singapore, 6–7 August 2009.

Rokka, J., Auriacombe, B., Arnould, E., & Sitz, L. (2023). Dynamics of convivial affective atmospheres. *Annals of Tourism Research*. https://doi.org/10.1016/j.annals.2023.103601

Rosetti, G. (2023). Conceptualising participant observations in festival tourism. *Current Issues in Tourism*. https://doi.org/10.1080/13683500.2023.2214850

Rothenberg, S., Hull, C. E., & Tang, Z. (2012). The impact of human resource management on corporate social performance strengths and concerns. *Business & Society*, *56*(3), 391–418. https://doi.org/10.1177/0007650315586594

Rusbult, C. E., Finkel, E. J., & Kumashiro, M. (2009). The Michelangelo phenomenon. *Current Directions in Psychological Sciences*, *18*(6), 305–309.

Santoso, H. B., Wang, J. C., & Windasari, N. A. (2022). Impact of multisensory extended reality on tourism experience journey. *Journal of Hospitality and Tourism Technology*, *13*(3), 356–385. https://doi.org/10.1108/JHTT-01-2021-0036

Sassler, S., & Lichter, D. T. (2020). Cohabitation and marriage: Complexity and diversity in union-formation patterns, *Journal of Marriage and Family*, *82*(1), 35–61.

Séraphin, H. (2023). Speed dating events: Introducing 'Special interest and meso-adultainment events' as a new type of event to existing Literature. *Journal of Convention & Event Tourism*. https://doi.org/10.1080/15470148.2023.2209341

Séraphin, H., & Yallop, A. (2023a). The marriage à la mode: Hospitality industry's connection to the dating services industry. *Hospitality Insights, 7*(1), 7–9.

Séraphin, H., & Yallop, A. (2023b). Rethinking the relationship between the dating services and the hospitality industry through speed dating events: Towards a partner ecosystem strategy, 3rd edition conference Modern trends in business hospitality & tourism, May 4th–6th, Babes-Bolyai University, Romania.

Sexton. (2022). Retrieved from https://www.earth.com/news/loneliness-is-a-global-health-issue-that-must-be-addressed/

Shabana, K. M., Buchholtz, A. K., & Carroll, A. B. (2017). The institutionalization of corporate social responsibility reporting. *Business & Society*, *56*(8), 1107–1135. https://doi.org/10.1177/0007650316628177

Staszak, J. F. (2018). Interview with Patrice Leconte, director of the Bronzés trilogy. *Via Tourism Review*. https://doi.org/10.4000/viatourism.3295

Statista. (2023). Singles worldwide. Retrieved from https://www.statista.com/topics/999/singles/#topicOverview

Stites, J. P., & Michael, J. H. (2011). Organizational commitment in manufacturing employees: Relationships with corporate social performance. *Business & Society*, *50*(1), 50–70. https://doi.org/10.1177/0007650310394311

Sweet, S. (2015). Editorial special issue. *Teaching Sociology*, *43*(2), 91.

Tantanatewin, W., & Inkarojrit, V. (2018). The influence of emotional response to interior colour on restaurant entry decision. *International Journal Hospitality Management*, *69*, 124–131.

Tasci, A. D. A., & Semrad, K. J. (2016). Developing a scale of hospitableness: A tale of two worlds. *International Journal Hospitality Management*. https://doi.org/10.1016/j.ijhm.2015.11.006

Tews, M. J., Michel, J. W., & Allen, D. G. (2014). Fun and friends: The impact of workplace fun and constituent attachment on turnover in a hospitality context. *Human Relations, 67*(8), 923–946. https://doi.org/10.1177/0018726713508143

The Chatty Café Scheme. Retrieved from https://thechattycafescheme.co.uk/

Turowetz, J., & Hollander, M. H. (2012). Assessing the experience of speed dating. *Discourse Studies, 14*(5), 635–658.

Upasani, S., Srinivasan, D., Zhu, Q., Du, J., & Leonessa, A. (2023). Eye-tracking in physical human–robot interaction: Mental workload and performance prediction. *Human Factors*. https://doi.org/10.1177/00187208231204704

Van der Meij, L., Demetriou, A., Tulin, M., Mendez, I., Dekker, P., & Pronk, T. (2019). Hormones in speed-dating: The role of testosterone and cortisol in attraction. *Hormones and Behaviour*. https://doi.org/10.1016/j.yhbeh.2019.07.003

Van Niekerk, M., & Getz, D. (2019). *Event stakeholders*. Oxford: Goodfellow.

Xu, C., & Kahl, C. (2018). Holiday or no holiday! How much power do children have over their parents in determining travel mode and preferred travel destination? An explorative study in Medan, Indonesia. In Gursoy, D., & Chi, C. G. (Eds.), *The Routledge handbook of destination marketing* (pp. 354–364). London: Routledge.

Xu, W., Li, M., Lin, G., & Feng, X. (2022). The socialization of preadolescents in family holidays: A serial mediation model. *Tourism Management*. https://doi.org/10.1016/j.tourman.2022.104578

Yang, J., Liang, N., Pitts, B. J., Prakah-Asante, K., Curry, R., & Yu, D. (2023). An eye-fixation related electroencephalography technique for predicting situation awareness: Implications for driver state monitoring systems. *Human Factors*. https://doi.org/10.1177/00187208231204570

Yeoman, I. (2013). A futurist's thoughts on consumer trends shaping future festivals and events. *International Journal of Event and Festival Management, 4*(3), 249–260.

Zacher, H., & Froidevaux, A. (2021). Life stage, lifespan, and life course perspectives on vocational behaviour and development: A theoretical framework, review, and research agenda. *Journal of Vocational Behaviour, 126*, 1–22.

Ziakas, V. (2019). Issues, patterns and strategies in the development of event portfolios: Configuring models, design and policy. *Journal of Policy Research in Tourism, Leisure and Events, 11*(1), 121–158.

Ziakas, V., & Costa, C. A. (2011). The use of an event portfolio in regional community and tourism development: Creating synergy between sport and cultural events. *Journal of Sport and Tourism, 16*(2), 149–175.

Ziakas, V., & Getz, D. (2020). Shaping the event portfolio management field: Premises and integration. *International Journal of Contemporary Hospitality Management, 32*(11), 3523–3544.

Zopiatis, A., Constanti, P., & Theocharous, A. L. (2014). Migrant labor in hospitality: The Cyprus experience. *International Journal of Hospitality Management, 37*, 111–120.

4 Conclusion

4.1 Reinforcing the Needs for Interactions…

It is tempting to say that the turn of the twentieth century has brought some challenges and difficulties for the tourism industry. In fact, the recent COVID-19 pandemic not only devastated the industry changing our current travel behaviour but also configured a new geopolitical landscape in the globe mainly marked by different consumption patterns (Lu, Wang & Zhang, 2022; Butler, 2023). The new normal started with proximity tourism as a new opportunity for a more sustainable agenda. In view of this, some voices applauded for the adoption of a more sustainable programme because of the economic crisis accelerated by the pandemic (Rogerson & Baum, 2020; Baum & Hai, 2020). However, in the time this agenda has ceded to new narratives and limitations, which captivated the attention of scholars (Yousaf, 2021; Gössling, Scott & Hall, 2020; Gowreesunkar, Maingi & Korstanje, 2024). The pandemic has prompted some long-dormant reformation in the industry which included new proximity destinations, the application of digital technologies in virtual tourism consumption, as well as the rise of single or solo tourism (Korstanje, Gowreesunkar & Maingi, 2024). Here we use the terms solo tourism and single tourism as interchangeable. Having said this, single (solo) tourism is not a new phenomenon. The term can be traced back to the end of the 1990s. Anyway, the phenomenon has gained considerable gravitation and traction in the fields of social sciences after the crisis generated by COVID-19. In this respect, solo (single) tourism should be defined as a tendency to travel alone. One of the methodological limitations to study the phenomenon is that solo-travellers are motivated by different purposes. At a closer look, solo travellers organise their trips by themselves without any type of companions or friends. Of course, their activities, though multifaceted, are centred on self-discovery and emancipation. Since some of these consumers look safest destinations the pandemic and health restrictions were the ideal scenario for the maturation of this niche (Sun et al., 2023; Jonas, 2022). What is more important, from it outset sociology has interrogated the tourist experience. As discussed in the first part of the book, sociology has been based

DOI: 10.4324/9781003502975-4

on a negative connotation of tourism. This pejorative viewpoint came from the French philosophy which demonised leisure activities as hedonist selfish behaviour. Beyond any discrepancy, sociology provided a fresh background to understand the role played by authenticity in the social imaginary. As a limonoid process, tourism consumption inscribes in a conceptual paradox. The tourist looks to get authentic experiences which in time are systematically standardised and homogenised. Although interested in the question of *the play*, the first sociologists were a bit sceptical concerning the expansion of tourism. In part, tourists look to be exceptional persons, or at least fill in a new role. Per their viewpoint, the expansion of tourism was conducive to the degradation of trust and social ties. Conceived as a postmodern (capitalist) activity, tourism aligns with autonomy, individualism, selfish consumption, hedonism and indifference. This begs a complex question: *Is tourism a social force or simply a service-related industry?*

Sociologists (like the calibre of Dean MacCannell (1973, 1976) John Urry (2002), Daniel Boorstin (1964) or Kevin Meethan, (2006) acknowledged that tourism should be seen as something more complex than a mere industry, but they emphasised the solitary and selfish character of tourism consumption. In industrial life, social solidarity has set the pace to mass consumption and individualism. Tourism is not good or bad – in the strictest sense of the word – but it reflects the mainstream values of society. Alienated or not, tourists look to consume outstanding (fabricated) experiences performed in a dream-world. Hence phantasy, play and exceptionalism are key factors to understand the vulnerability of tourism consumption. In such a process, the 'Other' not only is negated but also adjusted to the consumers' desires. Tourism sociology has divided in two main theoretical families; those who argue that tourism sublimates social frustrations into a coherent ideological narrative, and those who valorise tourism as a transformer of special geography. Besides, the expansion of global capitalism has undermined the autonomy of nation-states before the global capital. For postmodern sociologists, cultures, persons and their lives are commoditised in the global market. In consonance with this, there would be a type of *cultural matrix* that impedes a real engagement of tourists with locals or even with other tourists. Sociological theory has eloquently asked for the following axiom: why do tourists show antipathy or indifference to interacting with other tourists? This part combines the vision of various voices which – though critical – are helpful to understanding solo (single) tourism. Today different studies and theories offer an interesting diagnosis of solo travel or single tourism. The limitations of tourism sociology to examine social engagement have been shown by empirical research. This niche is mainly motivated by achieving safer practices for travelling without caring about the interaction with others. In the second part of this book, we decipher the discursive formation of solo tourism in the specialised literature. Centred on a discursive approach, this chapter explores the commonalities between sex tourism and solo tourism. Solo travellers are not lonely (anguished) people afraid from the locals. There is a type of symbolic stigmatisation revolving around the figure of solo travellers. Solo tourists are often married or have children. Their option is not based strictly on selfish forms of consumption. Rather, they engage with experiential moments of life to re-connect with the 'Other'. All this conceptual caveat not only is limited to the fact loneliness has not been duly discussed but also it is still under-researched. To some extent, loneliness has notably contributed to the formation and expansion of the economy of *romantic experiences or travel*. This economy is inserted in an eco-system that amalgamates different sub-industries or service sectors. This industry has profits of almost £150 million. For some reason, the tourism scholarship has a limited vision of romantic consumption. One of the aspects that define this niche remains covert for researchers and fieldworkers. At the same time, the features or demographic assets of solo travellers are overlooked by policymakers. The chapter gives a snapshot of the main assets of solo tourists as well as their underlying motivations. Having said this, the commonalities between Sex and Solo Tourism are stressed. While sex tourism derives from neocolonial practices where the 'Other (preferably the sex workers)' is certainly subdued, solo tourism allows genuine experiences with locals. The third part, complementarily, discusses *the meta-dimension of tourism and hospitality* which means the meta-service layer that adjusts to consumers' needs or tendencies. To put the same simply, the tourism and hospitality industries are generating changes in the contexts of persons, traversing across their biographies, cosmologies as well as career transitions. The tourism industry is playing a major role in people's lifespan. With a focus on sexual encounters and romantic relationships, the chapter places the current literature under the critical lens of scrutiny. The goals are twofold. On the one hand, it advances in a conceptual-practical dimension of the interplay between businesses and society. On the other, the chapter looks to understand loneliness, as a real phenomenon that greases the rails of the tourism industry. From its outset, tourism was considered as the counterpart of work. So to speak, lay people debated between working and leisure time. These borders have been blurred in the new normal. The intersection of leisure activities (or even the tourism industry) with the work-interface should be at least reconsidered. The chapter deals with emerging concepts such as Corporate Social Performance and Corporate Social Responsibility. The future of the tourism industry depends not only on the performance of their services or sub-sectors, but also on the correct understanding of the economy of romantic experiences, which include sex tourism, solo travellers, and romantic experiences.

4.2   What's Next?

Doubtless, tourism sociology has notably contributed to the advance of tourism research in the recent decades. The discipline, anyway, has been shaped by different sceptical narrative revolving around tourism. This so-called contradiction is mainly given by the influence of French philosophy, which demonised the leisure activities – even tourism – as naïve or business-centred practices. Despite of this, many sociologists have been turned their attention to the tourism industry. From its outset, the discipline focused on host-guest's relationships. At a closer look, sociologists have been concerned around a strange philosophical dilemma. While tourists look to face authentic experiences, they are enthusiastically embracing standardised (ideological) forms of consumption. From different angles, sociologists have emphasised on the crucial role played by authenticity in the tourist experience. From Boorstin to MacCannell, tourism was defined as a modern form of transport consolidated in the zenith of consumerist society. In this process, tourists rarely interact with others or locals in fact because it is subject to homogenised (fabricated) products resulted from a selfish behaviour. As a global force, tourism not only confronts with local cultures but also ethics. Having said this, the phenomenological world of tourists is cemented by the hegemony of digital media. What can be gazed upon or not is simply conditioned by a much deep cultural matrix. Some voices have alerted that the tourism practices are previously perpetuated by a long dormant neocolonial discourse where the 'Other' is eroticised, exoticised or negated. Tourism moulds local identities transforming radically the existent geographies. From generation to generation, the local culture is interpreted, and interrogated by the international tourist demand. In the first part, we have discussed not only the ebbs and flows of tourism sociology but also its ambiguous position regarding authenticity. The host-guest's interaction is influenced by specific patterns of consumption that affirm previous tourists' expectations. A review of the specialised literature says overtly that tourists are subject to exchanged narratives which are externally fabricated and offered. In this token, solo (single) tourism chrysalises an irreversible social decomposition centred on individualism and selfish behaviour. However, we offer an interesting background to hold that solo tourism has been successfully introduced to deal with some social maladies accelerated after the COVID-19 pandemic. Solo travellers not only engage with locals but also look new forms of self-discovery. Solo travellers look safest destinations so that they can potentiate their involvement with local cultures. Like virtual tourism, the pandemic engendered new forms of displacement and tourist experiences. Solo (single) tourism is part of a new tendency aligned with what experts dubbed as the economy of romantic loneliness. Here the term loneliness has received a negative connotation. As discussed throughout the second part of this book, loneliness tourism represents an unexplored market because of an extended stigmatisation process. Solo travellers are mistakenly associated to vulnerable women or divorced people. The evidence offered in this chapter goes in the opposite direction. Solo tourism traverses a dense net of demographic assets. It is important to mention that solo travellers are in quest of self-engagement with the 'Other'. At the same time, solo travellers can be identified with suitable modes of travelling where romanticism occupies a central position. What we know today about them is that more than 40% of the current demand is planning to travel alone in a moment of their lives. Their motivations also include self-discovery, meeting with locals, cultural heritage, rest and relax and expand cultural awareness. Solo travellers look to develop a climate of self-esteem through self-discovery. The current understanding of the academia on this new phenomenon is poor and marginally addressed. For that reason, we fill the gap offering readers an entire chapter that describes solo travellers´ motivations and characteristics. Of course, solo travellers situate as a growing niche that meets with specific applications in the websites. Nevertheless, solo tourism should be conceptually differentiated from similar forms of tourism such as romantic tourism or sex tourism. While sex tourism makes from sexual gratification its main goal, solo travellers focus on self-discovery. This tendency has been prompted by the COVID-19 pandemic as well as the restrictions to stop the virus dissemination. The COVID-19 pandemic not only changed the existent travel behaviour but also introduced regulation that demanded for safer modes of travel. Like virtual tourism, solo tourism denotes a marginal level of interaction with other groups. At the same time, solo travellers have shown higher levels of brand loyalty to the destination. The last part of this book deals with the problem of infrastructure and local services. We coin the term *meta dimension of tourism* to connote the levels of interaction among the different stakeholders in solo tourism as well as how it impacts on society. The chapter meets to respond basic questions revolving around the conceptual understanding of business and society. It also deals with romantic attraction and latterly relationship formation. It is noteworthy that future research in this arena should include the formation of suitable climates or atmospheres (for romantic meetings), personality of solo travellers, the contradictions or gaps in research, the gaps in the infrastructure, the lack of information or prejudices over solo travellers. We ponder a future agenda to study dating through the lens of hospitality and tourism. We look to expand the current understanding on human interaction through the type of service or product consumed. We toy with the belief that the concepts of Romantic Atmospheric Justice and injustice should be at least revisited. Second, the current literature does not suffice to explain the evolution and potential maturation of single tourism. The book is a personal attempt to improve the academic research in personality, psychology and social sciences regarding the power of authenticity and its intersection with the tourist experience.

References

Baum, T., & Hai, N. T. T. (2020). Hospitality, tourism, human rights and the impact of COVID-19. *International Journal of Contemporary Hospitality Management*, *32*(7), 2397–2407.

Boorstin, D. J. (1964). *The image: A guide to pseudo-events in America*. New York: Harper & Row.

Butler, R. (2023). Rethinking tourism: Why and who?. *Worldwide Hospitality and Tourism Themes, 15*(6), 602–607.

Gössling, S., Scott, D., & Hall, C. M. (2020). Pandemics, tourism and global change: A rapid assessment of COVID-19. *Journal of sustainable tourism, 29*(1), 1–20.

Gowreesunkar, V. G., Maingi, S. W., & Korstanje, M. E. (2024). Introduction: The interplay between tourism resilience and sustainability in the new normal. In Gowreesunkar, V. G., Maingi, S. W., & Korstanje (Eds.), *Tourist behaviour and the new normal, volume II: Implications for sustainable tourism development* (pp. 1–6). Cham: Springer Nature Switzerland.

Jonas, L. C. (2022). Solo tourism: A great excuse to practice social distancing. *African Journal of Hospitality, Tourism and Leisure, 11*(SE1), 556–564.

Korstanje, M. E., Gowreesunkar, V. G., & Maingi, S. W. (2024). Conclusion: Tourist behavior in the new normal—Emerging frontiers toward tourism resilience. In *Tourist behaviour and the new normal, volume I: Implications for tourism resilience* (pp. 273–278). Cham: Springer Nature Switzerland.

Lu, D., Wang, X., & Zhang, H. (2022). Tourism research on national parks and protected areas. In Luo, Y., Zhang, H., Jiang, J., Bi, D., & Chu, Y. (Eds.), *Tourism, aviation and hospitality development during the COVID-19 pandemic* (pp. 219–243). Singapore: Springer Nature Singapore.

MacCannell, D. (1973). Staged authenticity: Arrangements of social space in tourist settings. *American journal of Sociology, 79*(3), 589–603.

MacCannell, D. (1976). *The tourist: A new theory of the leisure class.* Berkeley: University of California Press.

Meethan, K. (2006). Introduction: Narratives of place and self. In Meethan, K., Anderson, A., & Miles, S. (Eds,), *Tourism consumption and representation* (pp. 1–23). Wellingford: CABI.

Rogerson, C. M., & Baum, T. (2020). COVID-19 and African tourism research agendas. *Development Southern Africa, 37*(5), 727–741.

Sun, Y., Zhang, J., Li, X., & Wang, S. (2023). Forecasting tourism demand with a new time-varying forecast averaging approach. *Journal of Travel Research, 62*(2), 305–323.

Urry, J. (2002). *The tourist gaze.* London: Sage.

Yousaf, S. (2021). Travel burnout: Exploring the return journeys of pilgrim-tourists amidst the COVID-19 pandemic. *Tourism Management, 84*, 104285.

Index

Printed in the United States
by Baker & Taylor Publisher Services